Vulnerability Assessment

The missing manual for the missing link

RG Johnston

Copyright © 2020 Roger G. Johnston
All rights reserved.
ISBN: 979-8-6524-1149-7

We cannot prevent what we cannot envision.
　　　　　　　　-- Kishore Mahbubani

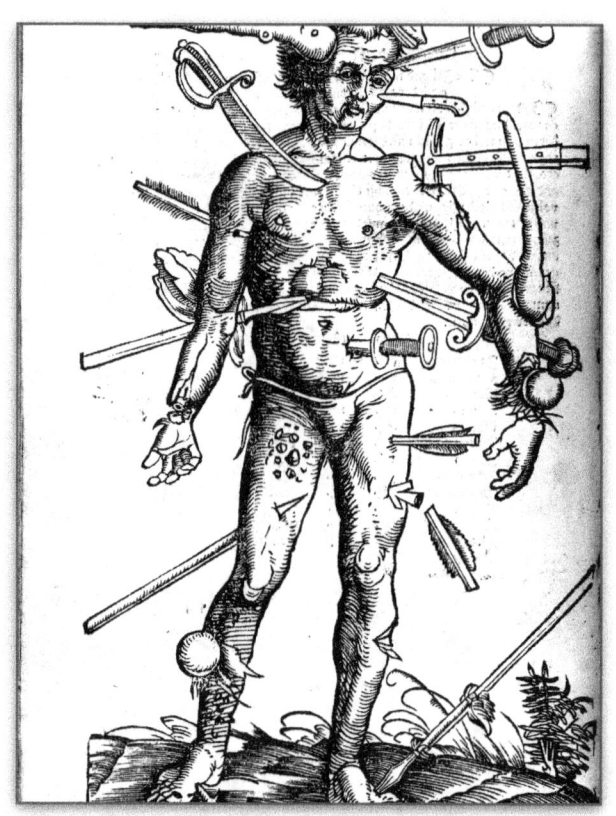

A bad day at the office?

This is an illustration of Wound Man from a 1517 book for surgeons. Wound Man might have benefitted from better Vulnerability Assessments.

Image Credits

All images in this book were either created by the author, or are in the public domain and originated before 1925.

Front Cover: *Vulnerability Assessment*, a non-artist's conception by the author
Back Cover: A portion of T*he Laughing Cavalier* (1624) by Frans Hals (1582-1666)
Previous Page: *Wound Man*, Illustration by Johann Ulrich Wechtlin from the 1517 book, *Feldbuch der Wundartzney*, by surgeon Hans von Gersdorff (1455-1529)
Page 1: *Weakest Link*, photo by the author
Page 9: *Bourbon Barrels Aging*, photo by the author
Page 21: Push 'n Snap Child Lock, photo by the author
Page 22: *Death of Harris*, France (1890-1900)
Page 37: *VA Pyramid*, by the author
Page 46: *Tres de Mayo* (1814) by Francisco de Goya (1746-1828)
Page 49: Sarah Bernhardt as Hamlet (1899), by Lafayette Photos, London
Page 61: *Denial of Peter* (1610) by Robert Leinweber (1845-1921)
Page 61: *In the Mirror* (1890) by Auguste Toulmouche (1829-1890)
Page 69: *Ashes* (1895) by Edvard Munch (1863-1944)
Page 70: Label from a bottle of Clark Stanley's Snake Oil Liniment (~1893)
Page 77: *Merry Party in a Tavern* (1628) by Dirck Hals (1591-1656)
Page 78: Keystone Kops from the 1914 film, *In the Clutches of the Gang*
Page 78: *The Fair at Montrouge* (1885) by Gabriel Boutet (1848-1900)
Page 86: *Target & Arrow*, a non-artist's conception by the author
Page 87: *Measuring Tape*, photo by the author
Page 92: *Risk Surface*, by the author
Page 97: *The Naughty Maid* by Ludwig Knaus (1829-1910)
Page 99: *The Bitter Draught* (~1637) by Adriaan Brouwer (~1605-1638)
Page 104: *Scorpion Under Glass*, photo by the author
Page 108: *The Cardsharps* (1594) by Caravaggio (1571-1610)
Page 129: *Simulated Seal*, photo by the author
Page 130: *Gator*, photo by the author

Contents

Introduction	1
1-What are VAs And What are They Not?	6
2-The Purpose of VAs	25
3-How to Do Effective VAs	29
4-Who Should Do the VA?	39
5-Brainstorming and Creativity in VAs	47
6-The VA Report	55
7-Cognitive Dissonance & Intellectual Humility	59
8-Sham Rigor & The Fear of VAs	67
9-Security Culture & Security Theater	74
10-Security Metrics, the Fallacy of Precision, and Marginal Analysis	83
11-Insider Threat Mitigation	95
12-Security Reasoning Errors	116
13-Attacks on Security Hardware	122
14-Other Security Tips	128
Appendix - Security Maxims	136
About the Author	170

Introduction

The greatest of faults, I should say, is to be conscious of none.
   -- Thomas Carlyle (1795-1881)

This book is an appeal to stop confusing Vulnerabilities and Vulnerability Assessments (VAs) with other things, and to start doing imaginative and effective VAs. Advice for how to do this is offered. Along the way, there are tips for having better security.

There's an old saying that security is only as good as the weakest link. If that's true, then VAs are not just the weakest link, they are often the missing link. This is very unfortunate. Not only is the lack of effective Vulnerability Assessments the main reason security fails, I believe it is also the #1 reason that when security does fail, it tends to fail *stupidly*.

There are many examples of security disasters where the failure to understand, acknowledge, and mitigate security vulnerabilities and attack scenarios was the underlying reason for failure. These examples include disasters such as the Trojan Horse (1184 BC); the Maginot Line (1940); Pearl Harbor (1941); the Isabella Stewart Gardner Museum art theft in Boston (1990); September 11th (2001); innumerable mismanaged White House fence jumpers; the Antwerp Diamond Centre Heist (2003); Hurricane Katrina (2005); Edward Snowden (2013); various IT data breaches including those at Target (2013), Uber (2016), and Equifax (2017); and the Covid-19

Pandemic (2020). [Katrina and Covid are probably more safety incidents than security since there was no malicious adversary. There were, however, plenty of incompetent insiders in both cases, and incompetent insiders represent a kind of insider threat.]

The ideas in this book are based on my more than 3 decades of experience as founder and head of the Vulnerability Assessment Teams at Los Alamos National Laboratory and Argonne National Laboratory, and as a security consultant for a wide range of physical security devices, systems, and programs. My consulting and R&D has covered the gamut of physical security applications including tags and seals, GPS, intrusion detection, access control, biometrics, cargo security, port and warehouse security, nuclear safeguards, election security, counter-intelligence, product tampering and counterfeiting, video surveillance, insider threat mitigation, Security Culture, medical device security, security device evaluation and technology review, embedded systems hacking, public relations after security or hacking incidents, and negligent security.

My experience is largely with physical security, though I have worked with microcontroller and IT issues, as well as physical security for data centers. Many cyber/IT professionals have told me that my ideas on security, insider threat mitigation, and Vulnerability Assessment are immediately useful in their line of work. Thus, I have reasons to believe that if you are more interested in cyber security or overall enterprise security than physical security, this book may still be of value to you.

Over the years that I have studied security, it has become clear that many organizations, as well as many security managers and other security professionals don't do Vulnerability Assessments, or at least don't do them well. Inertia, fear, denial, or fuzzy thinking are often the sources of the problem.

Why are good Vulnerability Assessments not getting done? Sometimes security managers are simply inexperienced or clueless about what a VA is and what it can do to improve their security. They may be hampered by sloppy terminology that is so common in security and/or they get VAs mixed up with exercises they or others call "vulnerability assessments" that really aren't. They many only think they are doing VAs.

Another possibility is that they are afraid to have security weaknesses pointed out. The concept of a VA does tend to engender fear and loathing among security managers. This might not necessarily be irrational cowardice; if a security manager or other security professional works for a pathological organization that doesn't tolerate speaking truth to power, this might just be self-preservation.

Then again, reluctance to conduct effective VAs can be due to over-confidence or arrogance, wishful thinking, or cognitive dissonance—all natural enemies of good security. [Cognitive dissonance is the mental tension between what we want to be true ("we have great security") and what is likely to be true ("it probably falls short of what is needed").] Inconvenient truths can be hard to accept, much less act on. Another possibility is that many security managers and organizations simply cannot envision attacks and security failures, so they don't focus on them. They can't think like the bad guys because they are too strongly entrenched in the role of playing the good guys.

A roadblock to effective VAs is thinking of security as a binary thing—we are either secure or we are not secure. This kind of mentality, where people talk about so called "gaps" in security, makes it difficult to accept the idea that there are likely an unlimited number of potential security improvements, many tweakable in nature. Security, after all, is a continuum, not a black and white matter. Another possibility is that security managers may get so caught up with bureaucratic busywork and the day-to-day details of providing security that they can't see the forest for the trees.

A (Security) Vulnerability Assessment is potentially one of the most powerful tools for improving any kind of security. It is important, however, to use effective Vulnerability Assessment techniques, to employ creative/resourceful personnel with the proper mindset, to think like the bad guys and let them (not the good guys) define the problem, and to avoid common Vulnerability Assessment myths and mistakes. It is also crucial to understand what a Vulnerability Assessment is and is not, especially because this is a common source of confusion.

Yet another common stumbling block for frequent and effective VAs is sham rigor, and the fear on the part of engineers, security managers, and organizations of subjective and creative methods for analyzing security, especially for critical security like nuclear safeguards or homeland security. As will be discussed in Chapter 8, this fear is wholly misplaced. In my experience, the best Vulnerability Assessments are almost always subjective in nature, though this does not mean that objective, formalistic, reproducible, and quantitative methods of analyzing security have no value.

Another impediment to VAs is that they are typically time-consuming and relatively expensive, even though they can often give more bang for the buck in terms of improving security than Threat Assessments or other techniques for analyzing security. This is especially true given that VAs should ideally be done periodically and iteratively from the earliest design stage through marketing and deployment of a new security product, system, strategy, or program.

This book can help with all the above impediments to good VAs. Even if you have a sophisticated understanding of VAs and do them effectively, this book might still be useful; it may offer some practical tips, fresh insights, strong encouragement, and/or thought triggers.

You have to be careful if you don't know where you are going because you might not get there.
-- Yogi Berra (1925-2015)

It is not necessary to read this book sequentially, though I would suggest reading Chapters 1 and 2 first before proceeding. The book is organized as follows:
- Introduction
- Chapter 1 – What are VAs and What are They Not?
- Chapter 2 – The Purpose of VAs
- Chapter 3 – How to Do Effective VAs
- Chapter 4 – Who Should Do the VA?

Introduction

- Chapter 5 – Brainstorming and Creativity in VAs
- Chapter 6 – The VA Report
- Chapter 7 – Cognitive Dissonance & Intellectual Humility
- Chapter 8 – Sham Rigor & The Fear of VAs
- Chapter 9 – Security Culture & Security Theater
- Chapter 10 – Security Metrics, the Fallacy of Precision, & Marginal Analysis
- Chapter 11 – Insider Threat Mitigation
- Chapter 12 – Security Reasoning Errors
- Chapter 13 – Attacks on Security Hardware
- Chapter 14 – Other Security Tips
- Appendix – Security Maxims

At the end of each chapter, there are discussion and thought questions for students or security professionals to ponder.

The Appendix contains a listing of over 200 of my popular Security Maxims. Just because many are deeply cynical and sometimes obviously tongue-in-cheek does not mean they are untrue. Ignore them at your own peril (and that of others)!

Chapter 1. What are Vulnerability Assessments (VAs) and What are They Not?

*The slovenliness of our language makes it
easier for us to have foolish thoughts.*
-- George Orwell (1903-1950)

Terminology is about more than just pedantic semantics. Words strongly affect and constrain how we think. In fact, I believe that the sloppy terminology so often used in security concretely interferes with much needed critical thinking. So let's be careful about how we use words!

Ich bin ein Berliner. [I am a jelly donut.]
-- John F. Kennedy (1917-1963)

All we know is, when you put these two words together, it's magic.
-- Scott MacHardy on his company's popular "Coed Naked" clothing line

---

Definitions vary a bit, but for our purposes here (and if you want to be precise elsewhere) it is useful to define a **threat** as who might attack, when, where, how (though only in a general sense such as theft, terrorism, sabotage, fraud, etc.), with what goals and resources, and the general probability of the adversary actually attacking in any given day, week, month, or year. The people who represent a threat are called the **bad guys** or the **adversaries**. A **Threat Assessment (TA)** is an attempt to predict the likely threats.

In contrast to a threat, a **vulnerability** is a security weakness that could be exploited by the threats in order to cause undesirable consequences. A **Vulnerability**

Assessment (**VA**) involves discovering and perhaps demonstrating these weaknesses but also ways to defeat a security device, system, or program, i.e., **attacks**. The VA will examine the design of the security, but also possible countermeasures, including changes to the design of the technology or to the use protocol.

The **use protocol** is the official and unofficial/informal ways that security products, technologies, or strategies are used. For security products or systems, this includes methods of procuring, shipping, storing, installing, inspecting, maintaining, removing, and discarding, as well as interpreting/reporting its status and training on its use.

It seems odd to some security managers that an effective VA should not just find vulnerabilities, but also include suggestions for, or maybe even demonstrations of attacks, countermeasures, and security improvements. The thing is, a VA that only finds problems and doesn't offer possible solutions is not going to be well received, and its lessons will not be learned. This is not to say that the recommendations arising from the VA are the final word. Security managers will rightly have their own ideas of what to do with the recommendations.

An **attack scenario** is a potential method and sequence of actions that could be undertaken by the bad guys to defeat security. VAs seek to discover not just vulnerabilities, but also potential attack scenarios.

A security or facility **feature** is some element of a security device, program, facility, building, or infrastructure. It should not be confused with assets or vulnerabilities.

An **asset** is something that needs to be protected from threats. Valuable assets can include (among other things) people, equipment, raw materials, products, services, money, museum artifacts, facilities, buildings, networks, logistics, communications, intellectual property, trade secrets, personally identifiable information, and an organization's reputation. The harm that might befall these assets includes theft, damage, sabotage, vandalism, adulteration, tampering, terrorism, espionage, or loss of privacy.

Consequences are the bad results of a successful adversarial attack. Organizations and security managers typically underestimate the severity of both the potential immediate damage, as well as the long-term and ripple-effect damages.

Risk is the probability-weighted cost of loss or harm. A **Risk Assessment (RA)** attempts to identify and perhaps quantify risks. The assets to protect, consequences of security failures, VAs, and TAs are all important inputs to RAs.

Risk Management is a process of mitigating or eliminating risk by deciding on priorities like what to protect, how to protect it, and how to deploy security resources. Risk Management requires many inputs, including those from VAs, TAs, RAs, as well as information about prioritization of assets, consequences of security failures, estimation of probabilities, chosen security strategies, resources available, the nature of personnel involved with security, security and facility features, the organization's risk appetite, and other parameters. Effective, real-world Risk Management utilizes value judgements, objective analysis, subjective analysis, experience, expertise, intuition, modeling, statistics, and hunches.

It is critical to realize—which many security professionals and business executives seemingly do not—that vulnerabilities are not threats. Vulnerabilities are also not assets to protect, nor are they risks, security or facility features, or attack scenarios (though these things may have an impact on our vulnerabilities).

When the term "vulnerability" gets hijacked to mean something else, as often happens, it becomes very difficult to talk and think about vulnerabilities. There simply aren't any good alternative terms in English. "Security gaps" is a wholly misleading term (as discussed in the Introduction) because it encourages a flawed binary view of security whereas security is actually a continuum. Similarly, "security flaws" or "security defects" are, in my view, too accusatory and value-ladened terms to be good replacements for "vulnerabilities".

A related kind of confusion occurs when—as is quite common—VAs get confused with TAs, RAs, Risk Management, or other techniques for analyzing security discussed

What are VAs?

in this chapter. These are all quite different activities. Sloppy use of these concepts and terms is dangerous.

Just so we are clear on all this, let's think about an example. Consider protecting a bourbon distillery. The stored and aging barrels of bourbon are <u>assets</u> to protect, not <u>vulnerabilities</u> just because the bad guys may want to attack or steal them. The company's good reputation is also an asset worthy of protecting, as are its financial assets and trade secrets.

One possible <u>threat</u> to the distillery might be criminals or terrorists wanting to steal or tamper with the bourbon, or damage the facilities, using outsiders, insiders, or both. Possible vulnerabilities might include the facility being poorly designed for security, intrusion detectors that are easy to spoof or tamper with, a failure to lock doors, bad fire suppression (as a security, not safety issue) since bourbon is highly flammable, poor insider threat mitigation, absent or ineffective training of employees about social engineering, insufficient periodic background checks, weak financial controls, a general failure to keep computer anti-malware up to date, and a non-secure chain of custody for procuring hardware, software, and ingredients.

The attack scenarios are the hypothetical, detailed methods and procedures that the adversaries might use to attack the facility, such as deploying firearms, bribing insiders, picking locks, stealing cargo, tampering with ingredients or the finished product, or hacking the company's computers or website.

The gates in the distillery fences are some of the brewery security and infrastructure features, but not vulnerabilities in and of themselves. If combined with an attack scenario, however, they might form part of a vulnerability if the gates are poorly designed, installed, maintained, or operated. Similarly, the company's website is not a vulnerability, it is merely a feature (or asset) that could be hacked Hopefully, somebody is doing a Risk Assessment for the distillery, and is managing the risks, meaning trying to reduce or eliminate those that make sense, and making preparations for recovery should a attacks occur, i.e., doing Resiliency and Recovery Planning.

It is not enough for a man to know how to ride. He must also know how to fall.
-- Mexican Proverb

Effective VAs are critical because we can't really prevent attacks that we haven't envisioned. We can't even meaningfully test, model, predict, evaluate, or counter vulnerabilities or attack scenarios that we haven't envisioned. VAs are all about imaginatively envisioning security vulnerabilities and possible attack scenarios by thinking like the bad guys. The non-VA techniques discussed below are often not particularly good at doing this. Unlike VAs, they rarely mimic the thought processes of the bad guys. To best predict what the bad guys might do, you have to think like they do and go through a similar mental process of discovering vulnerabilities and possible attacks.

The non-VAs described below, while often confused with VAs, may still be well worth doing. They might shed some light on your security and reveal <u>some</u> of its vulnerabilities, but they are typically not as effective at finding security vulnerabilities and attack scenarios (or thinking deeply about your security) as a good VA.

Threat Assessments (TAs): As mentioned above, a TA is an attempt to determine the most likely adversaries, their characteristics and goals, and their mode of attack in a general sense. Despite limitations, TAs are definitely worth doing: You can't design your security to effectively counter the bad guys, or do a good job with Risk Management, if you don't understand who they are, what motivates them, what they are capable of, and the probability they will attack.

What are VAs?

While TAs are essential, they are not silver bullets nor are they as effective as VAs at improving your security. If you analyze all the examples of security failures given in the second paragraph of the Introduction, you will probably find that they were mostly due to the failure to understand vulnerabilities and attack scenarios, not a failure to understand the threats or consequences of attacks. The threats and consequences were mostly or entirely understood.

Generally speaking, VAs give you more "bang for the buck" than TAs. The reason is that if you understand and mitigate many of your vulnerabilities, your security may be in good shape even if you get the threats all wrong, which is quite possible because judging threats often involves a lot of speculation about unseen (and maybe non-existent) adversaries and their agendas. Conversely, if you thoroughly understand your threats, but have no clue at all about your vulnerabilities or how you are susceptible to specific attacks, you are probably in trouble because you will not know what attacks will look like in detail, or how to prevent and mitigate them.

Unfortunately, what people mean by a TA is often just a superficial list of terrorists and criminals (or other kinds of bad guys) who have attacked the organization or similar organizations in the past. It may also include speculation on likely attackers who have not yet attacked. Many TAs lack substantial, realistic analyses of threats.

TAs traditionally tend to be mostly reactive to past security incidents, and focused on the past. VAs, in contrast, are usually more proactive and more about the future; they are focused on trying to predict what has not yet occurred. Being proactive with security is always more effective, but also more challenging, uncertain, and politically dangerous than being reactive. Another advantage of VAs over TAs is that the vulnerabilities, attack scenarios, and proposed countermeasures identified in a VA can often be demonstrated, tested, or eliminated. This is rarely possible for threats.

"Bad guys attack and good guys react" is not a viable security strategy.
-- old proverb

Perhaps a key reason why many organizations focus on TAs instead of VAs is that TAs are a lot easier to do, and tend to give consistent results. Most organizations face a relatively modest number of likely threats, many that are fairly easy to anticipate. There are, however, usually several orders of magnitude more vulnerabilities than threats for any given organization or security product.

Another perceived problem is that VAs are not very reproducible. Different Threat Assessors will typically find more or less the same obvious threats. In my experience, however, different Vulnerability Assessors (VAers) often find quite different vulnerabilities. The same VAers, re-examining security a second time, will find new vulnerabilities they missed the first time. This can be very uncomfortable or even scary to security managers, security engineers, and senior executives who crave certainty. They may consequently conclude (incorrectly) that VAs therefor lack rigor or value.

Another reason that TAs may be viewed more favorably than VAs is because identifying vulnerabilities is often taken to be an implied criticism of a security program, even though vulnerabilities are always present in large numbers. Citing threats, however, is rarely taken as criticism. And whereas "shooting the messenger" is a big problem for Vulnerability Assessors, it is almost never an issue with TAs.

A thorough understanding of vulnerabilities requires a comprehensive appreciation of the exact, local details of the facility, security program, or application. (With security, the devil is always in the local details.) With threats, on the other hand, security experts with no knowledge of your particular security application or organization can still usually do a competent job of identifying many of your threats.

Another reason why people often (unfortunately) prefer TAs over VAs is that vulnerabilities often take more imagination to recognize than threats, and require thinking like the bad guys. Imagination and creativity are characteristics that are often not the strong suit of bureaucrats, managers, personnel with military and police backgrounds, engineers, security professionals, and others in large organizations. These types of people often have a very different mindset than do the nefarious adversaries.

Risk Assessments: An RA attempts to identify and quantify risks. It needs findings from both a TA and a VA, plus numerous other inputs. An RA cannot be the same thing as a VA because a VA can't decide overall risk probabilities or what level of risk is acceptable. Sometimes, what is called an "RA" is acutally a VA, TA, or a software-based Security Survey.

Security Surveys: A Security Survey involves walking through the infrastructure, facility, or building of interest, traditionally with a checklist in hand. Often this checklist is prepared primarily by the security manager(s) responsible for the security. In practice, the Security Survey checklist is often composed primarily of generic, boilerplate items taken from generic Security Survey checklists (which is less effective than custom Security Surveys).

The typical goal of a Security Survey is to see if the security measures planned for the organization, facility, or infrastructure are actually being implemented, and if they are being implemented effectively. For example, are the doors that are supposed to be locked really locked? Is the security guard at his/her station and fully alert? Are the motion detectors working? Is the anti-malware software up to date?

You can observe a lot by just watching.
-- Yogi Berra (1925-2015)

Security Surveys can be very important tools for improving the implementation of security measures. As such, they are very much worth doing, and worth doing often. They can turn up important surprises, and beneficially encourage "management by walking around"—always a good practice. They are also relatively inexpensive and noninvasive.

The limitation with Security Surveys is that—unlike VAs—they do not usually uncover previously unrecognized vulnerabilities or suggest new countermeasures. With their binary, checklist mentality, Security Surveys do not encourage fresh, independent, deep, or creative thinking about security vulnerabilities and attack scenarios, especially needed when local conditions have changed. They encourage the security manager conducting the Security Survey to think like a good guy, not view the situation from the perspective of a bad guy. When they simply become a bureaucratic exercise in mindlessly checking the boxes, they fade to irrelevance.

Too often with a Security Survey, the existing security practices, strategies, infrastructure, hardware, software, and personnel come to define the security problem in the mind of the security manager. This is undesirable because the unfortunate reality about security is that the bad guys are the only ones who truly get to define the problem.

Security Audits: A Security Audit involves checking to see if the organizational or infrastructure security is in compliance with (usually high-level) security rules, regulations, laws, policies, standards, and guidelines. Sometimes it also involves reviewing the merits or language of the local or low-level security rules and policies.

Security Audits do not usually turn up new, profound vulnerabilities, provide substantial insights into security issues, or encourage independent, creative thinking about security. Security Audits also do not encourage thinking like the bad guys. They are focused on thinking about security like a good guy and mostly as a bureaucrat. Moreover, Security Audits tend to encourage Compliance-Based Security. This often results in poor security, as discussed in Chapter 9.

Physical Security Assessments: The terminology here is vague. A "Physical Security Assessment" can be pretty much anything, but often is a type of software-based Security Survey for physical security, plus some generalized tips for having good security. Again, these are not truly Vulnerability Assessments.

Post-Incident Security Review: Typically, the main purpose of an investigation after a serious security incident is to fix blame and identify scapegoats. Such "witch hunts" rarely results in fundamental improvements. The approach is usually highly reactive, despite lip service to being proactive about security. The intense focus on the one specific attack scenario that led to the incident means that other vulnerabilities and potential attack scenarios receive insufficient attention.

Software Tools: Many organizations use software tools for doing infrastructure security assessments, sometimes including Vulnerability Assessments. These tools are often tweaked for certain industries, such as the chemical industry, transportation, utilities, education, nuclear, etc.

These software tools typically are more a form of Security Survey than a VA. They often include some general security issues that security managers should consider, and questions they should ask. The user of the software program may be asked to input relative semi-quantitative rankings or estimates of probabilities for use in matrices.

These software tools can be a useful place to start in doing an infrastructure VA. They may provide some ideas about what issues need to be considered. They are not, however, particularly effective tools for finding vulnerabilities in specific situations; they are simply too generic. Most vulnerabilities, and most effective countermeasures, depend critically on details of the specific organization or infrastructure in question, its location, personnel and their training, the specific adversaries, and other local factors. The "cookie cutter" approach to security that these software programs encourage is not conducive to good security.

Another common problem with software VA tools is that the people who write or provide input to these generic software programs usually have some security expertise, but typically lack a history of doing true VAs. They may be experienced with TAs and overall Risk Management, knowledgeable about common security practices and best practices, and/or familiar with choosing and integrating security products. They are often, however, not the creative, hacker types needed to find vulnerabilities and devise effective countermeasures. They may not think intuitively like the bad guys. Sometimes they are not even all that familiar with the industrial sectors their software program is focused upon.

Penetration Testing and Software Scanning (for cyber security): Pen Testing and Software Scanning can be useful for mimicking the automated attacks that cyber adversaries may attempt to use against web pages, APIs, networks, and apps. As such, they are definitely worth doing. Their main limitations are that they don't routinely uncover new vulnerabilities, nor can they typically test your security against attacks you haven't envisioned. Some of the new Artificial Intelligence scanning software may be starting to do a better job with the latter, but are currently no substitute for thoughtful Vulnerability Assessors.

Penetration Testing (for physical security): This kind of "testing" involves trying out one or a small number of (usually frontal) physical attacks to gain unauthorized entry. It is very difficult to make these tests realistic, to explore a large number of vulnerabilities and attacks, or to mimic contributions from insiders. The tested attacks are often not very imaginative or close to what resourceful adversaries would actually do. If the simulated attackers fail to succeed, this often creates a false sense of security in the organization. One advantage, however, of penetration testing is that it can keep security officers engaged and interested.

Red Teaming: In the good old days, i.e., the Cold War where we all thought we would die horribly in a nuclear conflagration, "Red Teaming" meant doing a Vulnerability Assessment. In recent years, however, the term has been hijacked—as so often happens in security—and now typically means something closer to a one-off testing of one kind of attack, particularly penetration testing for physical security. Like penetration testing, Red Teaming may be worth doing, but it can cause distractions, focus on too few vulnerabilities and attacks, is difficult to make realistic, and can lead to a false sense of security if the limited "Red Team" attack fails.

Field Readiness Testing, Acceptance Testing, User Testing, Ergonomic Testing, and Environmental Testing: These techniques are often applied to new security products. While they are definitely worth doing and their findings can have implications for security vulnerabilities and attack scenarios, they are not particularly proficient at finding them.

Design Basis Threat: Despite the gibberish-sounding name, Design Basis Threat (DBT) is based on a very common-sense idea. DBT means designing your security to deal with the current, real-world threats. Though this ought to be self-evident, it is surprising how many security programs are operated without much thought as to the nature of the threats. DBT is often used to "test" nuclear security/safeguards, which is nonsensical, circular reasoning because DBT is, as a practical matter, essentially what is used to *define* the threat.

As its name might suggest, DBT is really more of a TA technique than a VA technique. It is also typically more attuned to helping to decide how to allocate security resources than to discovering vulnerabilities. The technique itself does not offer much in the way of practical methods for finding vulnerabilities. The whole process of how to recognize vulnerabilities is often glossed over in discussions about the DBT technique.

There are other serious problems with DBT commonly found in practice that are not necessarily fundamental, theoretical weaknesses with the technique. These include tending to focus too much on protecting physical assets (at the cost of ignoring more valuable assets like people, information, intellectual property, morale, customers' interests, and organizational reputation); letting the existing hardware, personnel, and security strategies define the security problem instead of the bad guys; having the analysis done mostly by bureaucrats and committees; being dominated by groupthink; phony rigor; and being reactive instead of proactive.

DBT is frequently obsessed with straightforward force-on-force attacks and often ignores more subtle attacks, including those based on the use of disloyal or compromised insiders. DBT frequently and dangerously ignores simple and cheap countermeasures when the attack probabilities are judged (rightly or wrongly) to be low or zero. Moreover, DBT analyses are often done by personnel with various kinds of conflicts of interest.

It's common for DBT to be used to justify the *status quo*. It tends to find that the current level of security is adequate to meet the threat, because the threat was essentially defined by the current level of security, rather than by the true threat.

DBT can suffer from the Fallacy of Precision—thinking that because we assign a somewhat arbitrary numeric ranking or value to the probability of a threat or attack that we actually understand it. (The Fallacy of Precision is discussed more in Chapter 10.) Though it often involves the use of rankings and estimated probabilities, DBT ironically sometimes engenders a kind of binary thinking about security—that a potential attack or type of adversary is either dealt with or not dealt with.

As with Security Surveys and Security Audits, DBT can be a useful tool for assisting with Risk Management despite its shortcomings in practice. It is just not typically a very effective VA tool.

CARVER Method: The CARVER Method is popular among security managers who work for government agencies, especially police departments and the military. CARVER is an acronym that stands for Criticality, Accessibility, Recuperability, Vulnerability, Effect, and Recognizability. It was developed by U.S. Special Forces during the Vietnam War to help decide which targets had the highest priority for attacking.

The CARVER Method provides a logical, semi-quantitative way to judge how to allocate security resources by considering the value of a given target. Basically, targets (i.e., assets) are assigned estimated scores for the 5 attributes of Criticality, Accessibility, Recuperability, Vulnerability, Effect, and Recognizability. These relative rankings are placed in a table or matrix. The assets that score highest get the most attention and resources devoted to protecting them because presumably they are the targets of greatest interest to the bad guys.

Though it is often discussed as if it were a Vulnerability Assessment technique, the CARVER Method is actually a Risk Management tool for deciding how to allocate security resources. It has little to teach about how to discover vulnerabilities or design effective countermeasures. It often suffers from the Fallacy of Precision (discussed in Chapter 10), and the choice of weighting is not as rigorous as implied.

One strength, however, of the CARVER Method is that it focuses on the security problem from the perspective of the attacker more than many other techniques. Moreover, the CARVER Method places a strong emphasis on resilience and recovery after an attack. This is often missing in other security assessment techniques, including many VAs.

Delphi Method: The Delphi Method was developed in the 1950s and 1960s as a systematic way to make decisions about complex issues. It entails procedures to iteratively poll multiple subject matter experts in a way that preserves minority viewpoints, while trying to converge the whole group towards a single, optimal forecast or decision.

The Delphi Method has merit for making single decisions such as "where do we put the new bridge?" or in forecasting complicated future events. It can potentially be useful for deciding how to field security resources once the threats, vulnerabilities, assets, consequences, and resources are fully analyzed. There is little evidence, however, that the Delphi Method is an effective way to find security vulnerabilities or device practical, innovative countermeasures. Indeed, the focus is on the internal mental process of experts coming to some kind of consensus, not on creatively thinking like the bad guys, or on discovering a multitude of previously unknown vulnerabilities, attacks, and countermeasures. If the subject matter experts have not carefully studied the security issues specific to the security application in question, their ignorance will prevent their expertise and consensus from being very useful. If they aren't very creative, we may end up back at the same old *status quo*.

Feature Analysis: Feature analysis involves looking at the current security or infrastructure features as if they were the vulnerabilities. An attempt is made to identify their security "gaps". As discussed above, this is not usually a very helpful approach.

Safety Analysis, Fault and Event Trees: Fault Tree Analysis (FTA) is a safety or diagnostic tool used to predict industrial and technology failures. It is based on the idea of using a model of logical AND and OR gates in conjunction with information or estimates for hardware failure rates, stochastic event probabilities, and cascading chains of occurrences to predict system failure. FTA is a useful technique for understanding the effect of simultaneous or sequential faults of a complex system, but it is not particularly good at finding the causes for these faults, or even in cataloging all the faults that are possible.

Event Tree Analysis (ETA) is a related technique for overall system analysis. It is based on a top-down logical model for tracing the likely failure consequences of a single initiating event.

FTA and ETA techniques are quite useful for Safety or systems engineering analysis. There are, however, of dubious value for security because adversaries tend to attack in a deliberate, targeted manner at the point(s) of greatest weakness, not in some stochastic (random) manner, or necessarily in ways that require technology failure. As with other Safety analysis techniques, however, both techniques can help inform Security professionals as to what facility and technology features warrant extra protection.

On the surface, Security and Safety seem to be closely related. In reality, they are quite different. The main difference is that there is no deliberate, cognitive, nefarious adversary in the case of Safety. It should therefore not be surprising that techniques for analyzing and improving Safety are not particularly helpful for Security, which is based on countering bad guys. The mindset needed to optimize Security differs from that of Safety. This is why it is unfortunate, for example, that the International Atomic Energy Agency (IAEA) and the U.S. Nuclear Regulatory Commission (NRC) have historically analyzed a lot of nuclear security and safeguards issues from the standpoint of Safety, using Safety experts.

A classic example of how a Safety perspective can harm Security occurred in 2012. In March of that year, there was a recall of 900,000 "Push 'n Snap" cabinet safety

What are VAs?

locks. These consumer products were meant to keep kitchen and other home cabinets locked so that young children wouldn't have access to hazardous cleaners and other toxic household chemicals. There were 140 reports of babies and toddlers defeating the locks, resulting in 3 (non-fatal) poisonings.

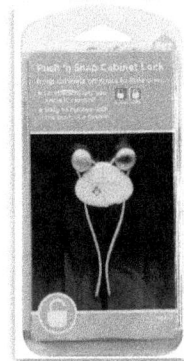

The problem was that the company thought it was selling a Safety product meant to protect kids. In fact, they were selling a Security product. Had they designed the product with the idea of countering the bad guys—in this case, malicious, trespassing babies and toddlers—they might have avoided the serious Security vulnerabilities.

All of this is not to say that understanding various Safety weak points and failure modes are of zero value in helping Security professionals understand what needs extra protection, the consequences of adversarial attacks, or how to prepare for recovery after attacks We certainly don't want Safety personnel to have no input on Security, or prevent Security personnel from commenting on facility Safety issues. Safety and Security personnel—who pay a lot of attention to facility, personnel, and enterprise details—should not remain silent if they see a problem in the other domain.

The key to getting better Security is to try to view things from the perspective of the bad guys. Despite the differences between Safety and Security, and that fact that Safety is not a good basis for analyzing Security, a Security mindset might nevertheless be beneficial for Safety. I have proposed that Security Vulnerability Assessment techniques can be applied to analyzing Safety by pretending there is a malicious adversary for Safety. This would not be an adversary that does deliberate sabotage—that would constitute a Security attack—but rather an adversary who passively, maliciously roots for Safety incidents to occur, with all their bad consequences.

MORT DE HARRIS (1824)

By visualizing an enemy to struggle against (even if imaginary), it may be psychologically easier to uncover Safety vulnerabilities. For more information on this concept, see "Adversarial Safety Analysis: Borrowing the Methods of Security Vulnerability Assessments", *Journal of Safety Research* **35**, 245-248 (2004), https://pubmed.ncbi.nlm.nih.gov/15288557/.

Design Reviews and Market Analyses: In a **Design Review**, there is a brief review of the design and engineering issues for a security product, system, technology, or program. Then, recommendations are offered for improving the design and the use protocol (how the product or technology is used).

I have found that many security managers and organizations are much more comfortable with a Design Review, than a Vulnerability Assessment. Arranging for a review of the design of a security product, system, strategy, or program is more familiar—and a whole lot less scary—than a blatant, close examination of security weaknesses. A Design Review is also cheaper and faster than a VA. The disadvantage is that fewer vulnerabilities, attack scenarios, and countermeasures will be identified in a Design Review than for VA, and the vulnerabilities, attacks, and countermeasures are typically not demonstrated, as they would be in a comprehensive VA.

While a Design Review will not permit as deep an understanding of vulnerability issues as a VA, it still offers the security manager or organization the opportunity to improve their security at modest cost in a short period of time. Moreover, in my experience, about half of the organizations that arrange for a Design Review eventually commission some kind of VA once they see the results and recommendations from the Design Review. Fortunately, much of the work that goes into the Design Review is directly applicable to conducting a later, more comprehensive VA.

An alternative to a Design Review is a **Market Analysis** where a new security product is compared to existing products. Potential applications and end-users are also identified. A Market Analysis can be a relatively non-frightening way to introduce some vulnerabilities and design issues, as well as potential countermeasures, without seeming to overtly criticize the security product or service.

The bottom line: sometimes a Design Review or a Market Analysis can sneak in information about vulnerabilities, attack scenarios, design issues, better use protocols, and other possible countermeasures in a more palatable way than a full-frontal VA. This can be helpful for security managers and organizations who are hesitant or fearful of learning about their security vulnerabilities, or think they don't have the time or funding for a true VA.

I don't think that anybody could have predicted that these people would take an airplane and slam it into the World Trade Center, take another one and slam it into the Pentagon, that they would try to us an airplane as a missile ... even in retrospect there was nothing to suggest that.
   -- Testimony of Secretary of State Condoleezza Rice to the 9/11 Commission. The statement was later proven wrong, including by the 9/11 Commission in its report. Various foreign governments, intelligence analysts, scholars, terrorists, and FBI personnel had warned about this scenario prior to 9/11, and something similar was outlined in Tom Clancy's popular 1994 novel *Debt of Honor*.

Chapter 1 Discussion and Thought Questions

1. Think about your local donut shop.
(a) What are 3 threats it is likely to face? Be sure to include in your Threat Assessment who the attackers might be, what they might want to achieve, what personnel and resources they likely have available, when they might attack, how (only in a general sense), and the general probability of adversaries actually attacking in any given day, week, month, or year.
(b) What are 5 vulnerabilities that most donut shops probably have?
(c) What are 3 likely detailed attack scenarios?
(d) What are some possible practical countermeasures to each of the vulnerabilities and attack scenarios you have identified?

2. How are Safety and Security similar, and how are they different? Why should safety experts not be in charge of security, as is historically common for nuclear security and safeguards, for example?

3. How can each of the non-VA techniques discussed in this Chapter (a) help shed light on some security vulnerabilities and (b) assist in improving security despite not really being VAs?

4. What are some of the reasons that people tend to get confused about the difference between Vulnerability Assessments and other kinds of security assessments and "tests"?

5. How would you explain to your CEO that "testing" security is not the same thing as identifying security vulnerabilities and thinking of ways to mitigate them?

6. Why are some people going to be better at finding vulnerabilities than others? What kind of attributes are good Vulnerability Assessors likely to have?

Chapter 2. The Purpose Of VAs

It's only when you look at an ant through a magnifying glass on a sunny day that you realize how often they burst into flames.
-- Harry Hill

Let's be clear. There are 2 purposes for a VA: (1) to improve security by discovering the security weaknesses, possible attack scenarios, and potential countermeasures, and (2) to provide input to an organization for Risk Management. Many organizations and security managers are confused about this simple idea.

Though it is unfortunately common, we should never view a VA as some kind of test to pass, especially for new security devices. It is not even clear what it means to "pass" a Vulnerability Assessment; it certainly cannot mean there are zero vulnerabilities. In my experience, security vulnerabilities are always present in large numbers for even relatively simple security products or programs. The fact is that a security device, system, or program can no more pass a VA than a person can pass an IQ test.

Similarly, a VA is not some kind of certification or endorsement. It should not be used to justify the status quo; claim there are no vulnerabilities; justify the R&D expenditures; or apply some kind of mindless bureaucratic stamp of approval.

A VA is also not fundamentally about quality control, acceptance testing, auditing, or helping the marketing department. It should not be about testing any of these things: compliance, performance, reliability, ergonomics, field readiness, environmental robustness of hardware, or response time. Certainly, some of these issues are very important for security and may have a bearing on security vulnerabilities and attack scenarios, but they are not the main focus or the fundamental purpose of a VA.

Critically, a VA should never engender warm and happy feelings. Good VAs should make organizations and security managers feel more concerned about their security, not more comfortable. That is the dismal nature of the security game.

A VA must never be used to praise or criticize security managers, vendors, contractors, engineers, security device designers, or frontline security personnel. The results of a VA should never be used in employee performance appraisals (though arranging for a legitimate VA should be rewarded). Weaponizing the findings of a VA simply encourages a culture of denying and covering up security problems, and will lead to a hostile or paranoid environment that makes VAs difficult to perform effectively, or even to do at all. Worse, it makes security the enemy of employees and others that the organization needs to buy into security. Weaponizing VAs is so dangerous that I sometimes insist as part of my consulting agreement that the client agree (at least verbally) to refrain from disciplining anybody as the result of inevitably finding vulnerabilities.

For similar reasons, the findings of a VA should never be used to generate security metrics. How frequently VAs are done or how robustly vulnerability findings and recommendations are dealt with, however, can be good metrics. VAs should not be used to test against some standard. (You can read more about problems with security standards in Chapter 8.)

The good news in all of this is that, in my experience, vulnerabilities are frequently easy and inexpensive to mitigate or eliminate once they are identified and acknowledged. (This, is usually difficult or impossible to do with a threat.)

Sometimes security managers or organizations will not bother to mitigate a vulnerability if they think that no threat is likely or able to exploit it. This is dangerous, however, because it is easy to overlook or underestimate adversaries. Moreover, we definitely do not want to ignore vulnerabilities that are easy and inexpensive to fix just because no immediate threat can be currently be identified that might exploit them. And even if we don't choose to fix a given vulnerability immediately, it is crucial to be aware of it should new information come to light.

Often, the discovery of vulnerabilities is viewed by organizations and security managers as bad news. This is an improper mindset! In fact, discovering vulnerabilities is good news. Vulnerabilities are always present in very large numbers, even for relatively simple security devices and programs. Finding a vulnerability means that something can potentially be done about it. This concept, however, is a tough sell to security managers ("Oh boy, we found another hole in the fence, isn't that great!") but it is the correct way to look at vulnerabilities and VAs.

Another common error is to think of a VA as a one-time thing, or something you do once every 3-5 years. In fact, VAs should be done continuously, both formally and informally. They need to be done early, often, and iteratively as new security products and strategies undergo development. It is much easier and cheaper to fix problems with a security device, system, or program early in the design process (even before the prototype stage) than later on. Iteratively re-examining the vulnerabilities after changes are made in security is important as well because the changes meant to mitigate existing vulnerabilities sometimes introduced new ones.

It may be useful to think of the technique of Vulnerability Assessments as having purposes beyond just security (and perhaps safety). Most executives, senior managers, and bureaucrats vehemently hate surprises and bad news. It has always amazed me, therefore, how few of them appoint what I would call a "Fire Marshal". This is someone who wanders around the organization looking for potential trouble of any kind (not just fires or security) before it happens, especially things currently off the radar. He/She listens to employees and contractors (especially low-level ones), asks questions, queries experts, and identifies where things could go south and what should be done in the way of prevention or preparation. This might involve looking for potential trouble that could arise in the areas of labor relations, racial/sexual harassment, bully bosses, illegal or unethical conduct, environmental disasters, community relations, health and safety, fire hazards, pandemics, security, hacking, insider attacks, product tampering/counterfeiting, corporate espionage, disruptive competitors, supply or shipping problems, public relations disasters, government interventions, etc.

While the Fire Marshal would be doing something closer to Risk Assessment than a pure VA, the ideas about how to do a good VA are still applicable. It is also worth noting that occasionally doing your own "Fire Marshal" analysis in regards to your personal life, career, education, and relationships might be prudent.

We are never prepared for what we expect.
-- James Michener (1907-1997)

Chapter 2 Discussion and Thought Questions

1. Explain why a Vulnerability Assessment is not a "test" of your security, and why it is dangerous to think this way. (If, for example, an organization or security manager views the VA as a test, are they likely to welcome the discovery of vulnerabilities?)

2. How would you convince an organization or security manager that the discovery of lots of security weaknesses is inevitable, and actually a good thing?

3. How would you deal with an organization or a security manager who insists on misusing or censoring the results of a Vulnerability Assessment, or commissioning one for the wrong reasons?

4. What can be done to prevent retaliation against Vulnerability Assessors or others who point out security problems? Does this kind of retaliation occur in your organization?

Chapter 3. How to Do Effective VAs

*We can not solve our problems with the
same level of thinking that created them.*
-- Albert Einstein (1879 -1955)

The Proper Mindset

The key to doing good VAs (and also to having good security) is, I am convinced, all about having the proper psychological mindset. This mindset requires, among other things, being skeptical about current security approaches, technologies, and assumptions; being able to do a mental coordinate transformation so that you can think like the bad guys; and being open to possibilities, imagination, and creativity. There is more discussion of the proper VA mindset in the next 2 chapters.

The problem is not the problem, the problem is your attitude about the problem.
-- Captain Jack Sparrow from the movie, *Pirates of the Caribbean*

Frankly, much of what I have to tell you in this book is little more than common sense—once you have the proper mindset about security and VAs. The problem with getting the correct mindset is three-fold. Firstly, the proper mindset is actually quite rare, even among people who are otherwise very intelligent and focused on security. Secondly, as Voltaire noted, the problem with common sense is that it is not all that common. Thirdly, even security managers and organizations with something close to the proper mindset and good common sense sometimes give nodding acceptance to the ideas in this book, but don't actually put them into practice.

Think about which one (or ones) of these 3 problems are limiting you and your security, as well as your organization and colleagues!

Getting or having the proper mindset about security in order to do a good VA is not easy. Let me give you 4 examples from my past of just how hard it is to have the proper mindset. The first involves a collaborator of mine who was a member of my Vulnerability Assessment Team. We were designing a novel, prototype security device as a way of demonstrating to the sponsor that there were other possible approaches to the poor commercial security devices they were using. My colleague was programming the microcontroller for our prototype device to include a PIN entry from a small keypad. He had the device beep with each digit entry, but unfortunately, a different tone was emitted for each different digit, 0-9. He totally missed the problem with this. An adversary hanging around the device could easily determine the secret PIN from a distance by hearing the tones! Now my colleague was a talented Vulnerability Assessor (VAer) who ordinarily had the proper security mindset. But when he began designing and building an actual security device, he entered "engineering" mode. He totally lost his security and vulnerability focus. It this can happen to an experienced VAer, it can easily happen to anybody!

The Mona Lisa was stolen because nobody believed she could be.
-- Francis Charmes (1848-1916)

Another security colleague of mine provides another example of how the proper security mindset for a VA can be fleeting. This talented individual was very knowledgable about ways to in defeat all kinds of locks, mechanical and electronic. The idea that most locks have serious, profound vulnerabilities was not news to him. So for locks, he had the proper VA mindset. Nevertheless, he was totally flabbergasted when I explained to him that we routinely defeat biometrics and other kinds of access control devices with simple, low-tech attack methods. He had simply assumed that these high-tech devices that he was not very familiar with would be difficult to defeat. The proper security mindset couldn't even be transferred to a different set of security devices!

The third example of how the proper security mindset is rare comes from all the security devices, systems, and programs I have studied, including those used for critical security applications like nuclear safeguards, counter-intelligence, pharmaceuticals, election security, and homeland security. Many of these clearly had little to no security in the design or in the recommended use protocol. This may well be because of a lack of proper mindset, though sometimes it is because customers are not really asking for security in the security products they buy, so why should the manufacturer build it in? Security is always more expensive and more of a hassle than not having security.

I have experienced a fourth example of the rarity of a proper mindset multiple times. Security managers are often astounded at how easily their security can be defeated with simple techniques, even when other aspects of their security are actually pretty good. Having been amazed once, however, the same security managers are just as amazed the next time around when other simple, unrelated attacks are demonstrated. The first incident of being amazed somehow does not inoculate security managers against a lack of skepticism about their security.

Black or White?

Once a good mindset is in place, along with the appropriate personnel (discussed in the next Chapter), a decision needs to be made about whether to do a White Box VA or a Black Box VA. In a **White Box VA**, the client or sponsor provides extensive technical details about the security device, system, or program—pretty much whatever the VAers request. In a **Black Box VA**, the VAers discover most things for themselves.

Black Box VAs are enormous fun and can be quite educational, but they are a huge waste of time and money. The fact is, the true bad guys will be able to figure out most or all of the sponsor or client's secrets—using insiders if necessary—because no organization can effectively keep secrets long term, anyway. The bad guys, however, will be able to obtain the necessary information cheaper and quicker than the VAers because they are not constrained by ethical or legal limitations. (Besides, as discussed elsewhere in the book, security is usually better when it is transparent, not based on "security by obscurity".) The bottom line is that a White Box VA usually makes the most sense.

The VA Process

The basic recipe for a VA is as follows:

Step 1, Study: Study the security device, system, or program to be analyzed. Fully understand how it really operates, not just how it is supposed to. Talk to the low-level users, not just the managers and supervisors who don't always fully understand how things actually work. Keep "Rohrbach's Maxim" in mind: No security device, system, or program will ever be used properly (the way it was designed) all the time. And maybe even the "Rohrbach Was An Optimist Maxim": No security device, system, or program will ever be used properly. (More security maxims are in the Appendix.)

Step 2, Play Around: Do some initial playing around with the security device, system, or program. To the extent possible poke it, perturb it, test it, and "kick the tires" to see how it behaves.

Step 3, BS: Start brainstorming ideas about vulnerabilities and possible attack scenarios. (Brainstorming and creativity are discussed in Chapter 5.) Anything goes! At the brainstorming stage, we do not worry about practicality.

Step 4, Play Some More: Play with the security devise, system, or program some more based on ideas generated in the brainstorming.

Step 5, Edit Attack Candidates: Edit and prioritize potential attacks.

Step 6, Develop Attacks: Partially or fully develop some of the devised attacks. This is for the purposes of determining the difficulty and feasibility of the attacks, as well as deciding which attacks might be worth demonstrating.

Step 7, Devise Countermeasures: Devise countermeasures and better use protocols with more brainstorming.

Step 8, Perfect Attacks: Improve or perfect attacks to be demonstrated.

Step 9, Demo Attacks: Demonstrate attacks or partial attacks you have chosen to demonstrate. Video documentation is often useful.

Step 10, Test Attacks: Rigorously test attacks you have chosen to demonstrate.

Step 11, Edit Countermeasures: Prioritize possible countermeasures and better use protocols. Improve or perfect them.

Step 12, Demo Countermeasures: Demonstrate countermeasures or partial countermeasures, and the recommended use protocols. Video demos often work well.

Step 13, Test Countermeasures: Rigorously test countermeasures and use protocols you have chosen to demonstrate.

Step 14, Write Report: Prepare the Vulnerability Assessment Report and other documentation of the VA. (About a third of my VA sponsors do not want any written documentation of the Vulnerability Assessment, just an oral briefing. This is more due to political and career risks than confidentiality/classification issues, and is *not* the sign of a healthy Security Culture!)

Step 15, Review: The VAers are brought back after countermeasures are deployed to see if they are effective and to determine what new vulnerabilities have been introduced as a result. This is because changes meant to mitigate vulnerabilities often introduce new (hopefully lesser) vulnerabilities.

Peer's Law: The solution to the problem changes the problem.

Keep in mind that the sponsor or client for a VA will often be unwilling to fund some or all of Steps 6, Steps 8-13, and 15. These tend to be the most expensive and time-consuming steps. The unwillingness to fund these steps may be about the time or money. It might also be the case that the sponsor or client does not want to be directly confronted by the reality of the vulnerabilities and attack scenarios by having them demonstrated to their face. They may also not want there to be a written or video record of successful attacks, so they may want to skip a formal Step 14.

Steps 10 and 13 involve rigorous testing. Even if the sponsor or client is willing to fund these steps, the testing itself is very problematic. Ideally, testing is done repetitively in a realistic, double blind manner in the relevant environment using careful controls. This can be extremely challenging to arrange, especially if the attackers face significant risk of harm. Moreover, it is difficult not to tip off security guards or other personnel about these tests.

VAs on tamper-indicating seals often used for cargo, nuclear safeguards, or election security are an instructive example. Invariably, the sponsor or client sends their absolute best seal inspectors to be part of the test, with the inspectors being aware it is a test so they are on heightened alert—not a very realistic situation compared to everyday security operations. To avoid being fooled, the inspectors will often claim that every seal they inspect has been spoofed or opened—something that could not be tolerated in practice. To deal with this problem, I usually need to give each inspector a quota on how many seals they could declare to attacked, but that is hardly realistic!

(Despite these problems, my Vulnerability Assessors and I have always managed to fool seal inspectors. Reliable tamper-detection is a largely unsolved problem for all but the most inept adversaries, despite what many manufacturers, vendors, organizations, and security managers claim or want to believe.)

One of the important things I have learned from numerous VAs is that the best ideas for vulnerabilities, attack scenarios, and countermeasures typically come late in the VA process, sometimes as you are writing the Vulnerability Report. You have to remain flexible and plan for this. Moreover, thinking about vulnerabilities, attacks, and countermeasures should not end when the VA is officially over!

Another lesson is to watch out for artificial or unrealistic constraints. The VA needs to be done holistically, not compartmentalized by component, sub-system, function, layer, or technical discipline. Many VAs are compartmentalized so that mechanical engineers look at the mechanical design, electrical engineers at the electronics, computer people at the software, etc. While using subject matter experts is fine, attacks often occur at interfaces and the vulnerabilities need to be examined from a broad, multi-disciplinary view.

It is critical that the VA not have artificial or unrealistic time or budget limitations, and not be constrained in regards to scope and what attacks or adversaries can be considered (as is common). There should also be no underestimation of the cleverness, knowledge, skills, dedication, or resources of likely adversaries.

It is especially important that VAs not be limited by the current understanding of threats. In theory, if no threat exists to exploit a particular vulnerability, it could be ignored. In practice, it is too easy to miss or underestimate threats, or they may change. Moreover, the recognition of a vulnerability or attack scenario that is unlikely to be exploited can lead to the discovery of others that <u>are</u> likely to be exploited.

A good VA will always find new vulnerabilities and attack scenarios. Any VA that does not needs to be discarded and new VAers found who are not incompetent or dishonest.

In doing a VA, it is important not to let the envisioned vulnerabilities define the attack scenarios. It is more like the other way around. Countermeasures proposed in the VA should include remediation/recovery after an attack and not just be about prevention, which is never perfect.

An effect VA should also be done in context to the extent possible, not is some idealized and unrealistic laboratory setting. Also, the good guys don't get to define the

35

security problem, and low-tech attacks are considered first because they are usually adequate, even against high-tech security. The potential role of insiders, especially disgruntled employees, must be carefully considered by VAers as well. (There is more on the Insider Threat in Chapter 11.)

> *The more sophisticated the technology, the more vulnerable it is to primitive attack. People often overlook the obvious.*
> -- Tom Baker as Doctor Who in *The Pirate Planet* (1978)

I am often asked if there is a good standard for Vulnerability Assessment. At least for physical security, I have seen nothing that helps much. Like many security standards, standards for "assuring" security effectiveness are often, in my view, overly simplified and written with the wrong security mindset using appalling bad terminology and sloppy reasoning. They also tend to be developed with far too much dominance by special interests. Currently, we have to be satisfied with our understanding of the general requisite attributes of a good VA. An effective VA, like pornography, is easy to recognize but hard to define.

Where do Vulnerability Ideas Come From?

There is something of a hierarchy of where ideas about vulnerabilities, attack scenarios, and countermeasures come from. I call this the "Vulnerability Assessment Pyramid". See the figure below. Ideas generated from considering the common issues at the bottom of the pyramid can have some merit, but are rarely very profound or effective at improving security. The issues at the top of the pyramid are much less common when people think about security, but usually generate the best ideas.

As suggested by the figure, the best way to do a VA is to undertake a great deal of creative discovery and analysis. Envisioning attack scenarios is the next best way to discover vulnerabilities. The common, but weak methods for thinking about security vulnerabilities at the bottom of the pyramid are either too reactive and non-proactive (past security incidents), or only tangentially on topic (threats and safety).

How to Do Effective VAs

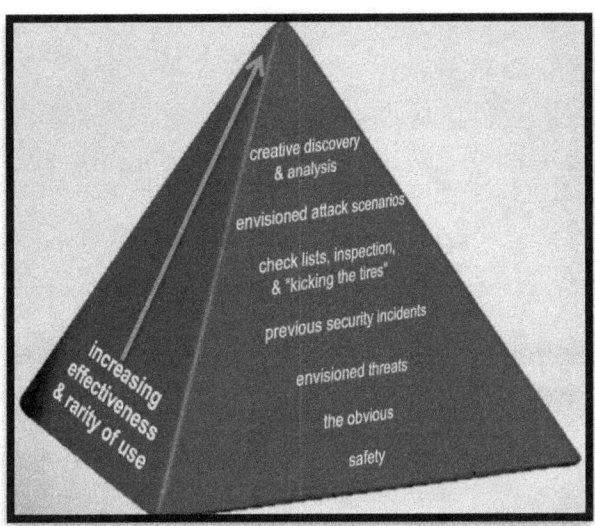

Since a VA is a "right brain" exercise in creativity, sham rigor needs to be shunned. It is a mistake to believe an effective VA process can be done in a rigorous, formalistic, linear, reproducible, or quantitative manner. Not all the vulnerabilities, possible attack scenarios, or potential countermeasures are likely to ever be found. The VA process is thus difficult to formalistically characterize, reproduce, or automate.

Everything you can imagine is real.
-- Pablo Picasso (1881-1973)

Chapter 3 Discussion and Thought Questions

1. Why is the proper security mindset so important for VAers? For security managers?

2. Think about which one (or ones) of these 3 problems, if any, are limiting how you, your colleagues, and your organization deal with security: (a) Not having the proper security mindset. (b) Missing basic common sense, at least to some extent. (c)

Having the proper mindset and good common sense but not actually implementing the necessary ideas.

3. Why are security managers often more comfortable with the methods at the bottom of the Vulnerability Assessment Pyramid than the top? What do you think can be done to get them to use the ones at the top more?

4. Why do security managers and organizations tend to want definitive, rigorous VA findings?

5. Which of the Vulnerability Assessment steps do you think are the most difficult? The most time consuming? The most expensive? The most requiring of specialized skills?

6. What are the advantages and disadvantages of White Box VAs versus Black Box VAs?

7. Why can known threats not be used to constrain our thinking about vulnerabilities and possible attack scenarios?

8. Why can the envisioned vulnerabilities not limit the attack scenarios being considered in a Vulnerability Assessment?

9. What makes a good Vulnerability Assessment?

Chapter 4. Who Should Do the VA?

Who naught suspects is easily deceived.
-- Francesco Petrarch (1304-1374)

One answer to the question of who should do Vulnerability Assessments is "Everybody!". All security managers and security professionals should continually be asking themselves, "How can our security be defeated?"

Not only that, but all regular (non-security) employees and contractors should periodically be asked how they think the organization's security could be defeated—not just how it could be better—and how they personally would attack the organization, with or without outsiders. Even if the answers are redundant or impractical, encouraging such thinking can help nurture better security awareness and a healthy Security Culture in the organization. (For more on Security Culture, see Chapter 9.) Even if an employee's or contractors' ideas are insane, they should be thanked and praised for their input.

(In the case of safety, employees should not just be asked how they could work more safely, they should be asked how they or their coworkers are most likely to get hurt or killed.)

Our enemies are innovative and resourceful, and so are we.
They never stop thinking about new ways to harm
our country and our people, and neither do we.
-- George W. Bush

Some security managers blanch at the idea of encouraging employees to think about vulnerabilities and how to defeat security. The fact is, there is little risk to this with loyal employees. And the disloyal or disgruntled ones are already thinking about attacks and security weaknesses, anyway, whether they ever act on them or not.

He that wrestles with us strengthens our nerves and sharpens our skill. Our antagonist is our helper.
-- Edmund Burke (1729-1797)

While everyone should be thinking about vulnerabilities and attack scenarios, ongoing informal Vulnerability Assessments are not a good substitute for formal Vulnerability Assessments done by security experts able to look at the organization and its security challenges with independent eyes. VAs done by external Vulnerability Assessors are almost always going to be more prescient than those done by insiders. Vulnerabilities are often obvious to outsiders. Moreover, insiders have an inherent conflict of interest, lack fresh insights into the organization, hopefully have already fixed any vulnerabilities they could recognize, and simply risk too much career-wise given the "shoot the messenger" problems often associated with pointing out security vulnerabilities.

My definition of an expert in any field is a person who knows enough about what's really going on to be scared.
-- P.J. Plauger

In many fields other than security, peer review is extensively used to improve quality and accountability. This is the case in science, mathematics, engineering, and medicine. But in security, we rarely have true peer review. This is unfortunate.

Thus, external VAs are better, but if VAs done by external Vulnerability Assessors are simply not an option because of budgetary issues or fear from higher ups, an internal, formal VA is the next best option. (Keep in mind, it is also possible to have both internal and external VA teams, perhaps working in staggered years.) How to choose an internal VA team is discussed below. First, however, let's think about how to select a good external VA team.

The old adage that "it takes a thief to catch a thief" has some merit for VAs. This isn't to say you should necessarily hire a bunch of felons to look at your security. What it does mean is that the VAers need the right attributes. They certainly should have the proper security mindset, as was discussed in the previous chapter. They should be psychological predisposed to finding security problems and suggesting solutions, and ideally have a history of doing so. "Assessors" who typically find few or zero vulnerabilities, and/or who concentrate on reassuring the sponsor or client that everything is swell when it is not are worse than useless.

In seeking an external VA team, always look for VAers with previous sponsors or clients who say that the Vulnerability Assessors made them think and made them uncomfortable. That is a good sign. Note, however, that many organizations and security managers do not like to be associated with the idea of vulnerabilities and Vulnerability Assessors, so they may be unwilling to give any recommendations about VAers, or even to acknowledge that outside VAers have taken a look at their security.

It is important that the VAers have a history of considering subtle and clever attacks, not just full-frontal and blatantly obvious ones. They should be able to think about insider attacks and insider assistance with attacks. The VAers should have a history of concentrating mostly on low-tech attacks because (in my experience) low-tech attacks almost always work against security devices, systems, and programs—even high-tech ones. Some consideration of high-tech attacks, however, is also useful.

One of the advantage of demonstrating low-tech attacks is that clients and sponsors take the related vulnerabilities more seriously. It is too easy for them to dismiss a high-tech attack as being "beyond the capabilities of our adversaries", even when such a claim is dubious.

In my experience, the best VAers are highly creative thinkers with a hacker and somewhat maverick mentality. They asked good questions. They tend to possess a suspicious, skeptical, or even cynical mindset that questions common assumptions, authority, and how things are done. The formal credentials of VAers may be less important than their mindset and attributes, but obviously at least some (but definitely not all) members of a Vulnerability Assessment team should be subject matter experts.

> *[One way] researchers sometimes evaluate people's judgments is to compare those judgments with those of more mature or experienced individuals. This method has its limitations too, because mature or experienced individuals are sometimes so set in their ways that they can't properly evaluate new or unique conditions or adopt new approaches to solving problems.* -- Robert Epstein

It is difficult to make a living as a Vulnerability Assessor for a variety of reasons. This is much more the case for physical security than cyber security. Thus, the external Vulnerability Assessment Team that you hire might not do VAs full-time. This is not necessarily a problem. Just be sure that they do not represent the other things that they are doing as Vulnerability Assessments when they are actually something else (as discussed in Chapter 1).

> *"Out of the box" problem-solvers have developed a series of habits to connect the dots effortlessly and trigger creativity frequently in order to solve problems elegantly.*
> -- Pearl Zhu

Let's turn now to forming your own internal VA team. Who should be on the team? You certainly want some internal security professionals, engineers, and subject matter experts. Just not too many. You are looking for people (not just security professionals or engineers) with a hacker mentality who are highly creative, resourceful, skeptical/cynical, questioners of authority, loophole finders, rule breakers, hands-on types, non-black-and-white thinkers, and smart alecks/wise guys. People who are narcissists, introverts, troublemakers, and who might ordinarily be considered your worst security nightmare are often a good choice to be on the VA team because they more closely resemble the bad guys. People skilled with their hands (e.g., artists, artisans, graphic artists, craftspeople, machinists, car mechanics) who are interested in details and in how things are designed and work are often useful as well, even if not security experts.

> *Extroverts are more likely to take a quick-and-dirty approach to problem-solving, trading accuracy for speed, making increasing numbers of mistakes as they go, and abandoning ship altogether when the problem seems too difficult or frustrating. Introverts think before they act, digest information thoroughly, stay on task longer, give up less easily, and work more accurately. Introverts and extroverts also direct their attention differently: if you leave them to their own devices, the introverts tend to sit around wondering about things, imagining things, recalling events from their past, and making plans for the future. The extroverts are more likely to focus on what's happening around them. It's as if extroverts are seeing "what is" while their introverted peers are asking "what if."*
>
> -- Susan Cain

If you have any Cassandras in the organization, be sure to include them on the internal VA team. Cassandras, from Greek mythology, are people who warn about security problems or other risks but feel they aren't being listened to. Sometimes they will attack an organization simply to prove they were right, but participation in the VA team can help neutralize this impulse. Stroking the egos of Cassandras is important, as is taking their concerns seriously. Putting them on the VA team is one way of doing this, plus it leverages their passion about risk and security vulnerabilities.

One of the advantages of drafting non-security people to be part of your internal VA team is that this encourages general employees to think critically about security. This sends the right message to employees, and is good for your Security Culture. Another advantage of using your own people for VAs is that any attack they devise will no longer seem cool to innovative hackers and (if they are aware of the attack) they may drop it from their potential arsenal.

You definitely want to avoid putting high-level managers, CSO's, and CISO's on the internal VA team, or anybody with authority who might dampen and suppress discussion, creativity, or the team's findings. You also want to avoid having too many engineers on your internal VA team, or letting an engineer lead the team.

The reality is that engineers don't typically get security. It is a completely different mindset. Engineers work in solution space, not problem space. They rely on conventional designs and focus on a good experience for the user and manufacturer, rather than a bad experience for the bad guy. They view nature or economics as the adversary, not people, and instinctively think about systems failing stochastically or due to bugs, rather than due to deliberate, intelligent, malicious intent. Flexibility of thinking or appreciating an adversary's viewpoint is often not engineers' strong suit.

Keep in mind that being intelligent does not automatically make someone think like a bad guy or be creative. Magicians and con artists know, for example, that technical people are often the easiest to fool because they tend to think logically and in a linear fashion. In contrast, magicians often fear children because they do not think that way.

For a good internal VA, it is absolutely essential that the internal VAers be protected from retaliation, and that they know that going in. Doing a VA for your own organization can be a threat to your career, or at least place real or perceived pressure on the VAers not to find substantial vulnerabilities.

There is an old adage that "a prophet is never honored in his own land." As I can personally attest to, there is a lot of "shoot the messenger" syndrome (retaliation) aimed at people who identify security problems and possible future attacks. Indeed, while vulnerability assessors are sometimes called "red teamers" (from the Cold War era), or "black hatters" (from cowboy westerns), they are also often called worse things that can't be repeated in polite company.

Who Should Do the VA?

> *Definition—Vulnerability Assessors: Wiseguy troublemakers
> who appreciate the value of nothing, especially hard work.*
>
> -- *Devil's Dictionary of Security Terms*

The problem of retaliation is one of the reasons that VAers should ideally come from outside the organization. Internal or external, however, VAers must be able to be independent and allowed to report whatever they discover without fear or retaliation.

There also can be no conflicts of interest. VAers certainly cannot be advocates for the security product or program under study, nor benefit from its implementation. The U.S. government, for example, is notorious for letting people with severe conflicts of interest comment on or even control the discussion about security vulnerabilities, assuming there even is a discussion. This has, in my view, led to some horrendously flawed security technologies, systems, and programs.

True friends stab you in the front.
-- Oscar Wilde (1854-1900)

Chapter 4 Discussion and Thought Questions

1. Think about which friends or coworkers you know who might make good Vulnerability Assessors. What is it about them that makes you think so?

2. Does your organization encourage employees and contractors to think about security vulnerabilities and attack scenarios, and share their ideas with management?

3. What are some of the risks of encouraging employees and contractors to think about security vulnerabilities and attack scenarios, and share their ideas? Is it worth these risks?

4. What ways can you think of to prevent organizations from retaliating against or discouraging employees and Vulnerability Assessors from pointing out security issues?

5. What are the advantages and disadvantages of using external Vulnerability Assessors?

Chapter 5. Brainstorming and Creativity in VAs

The best way to have a good idea is to have lots of ideas.
-- Linus Pauling (1901-1994)

The Creativity Mindset

As we've seen, a Vulnerability Assessment is essentially an exercise in creativity. You pretend to be the adversary and imagine what might be. You look beneath the surface and discover security weaknesses and possible ways to attack security that others have missed. You then devise and invent new countermeasures and use protocols.

Some security managers question the need for creativity in security. They believe their adversaries are not particularly resourceful or creative. This is always a dangerous assumption to make given that the bad guys have plenty of incentive because they may face a big payoff. If nothing else, they can always hire creative people, perhaps under false pretense. More to the point, the good guys have to be more creative than the bad guys because defense is harder than offense. The adversary needs only to discover and exploit one or a small number of vulnerabilities, while security managers have to manage and defend against all of them, including the ones they don't even know exist.

The only difference between the fool, and the criminal who attacks
a system is that the fool attacks unpredictably and on a broader front.
-- Tom Gilb

To a considerable extent, the creativity required for VAs is not much different from the creativity required for any other kind of problem solving. And researchers actually know a fair amount about nurturing creativity. The advice on creativity for VAs offered in this chapter is a mixture of these research findings and my own experience.

Vulnerability Assessment

I have found that it is easier to adopt the mindset of the bad guys by using certain aspects of Method Acting. This is an acting technique originally developed in Russia by Konstantin Stanislavsky. It eventually became popular in the United States in the 40's and 50's., taught by prominent acting coach Lee Strasberg. Famous Method actors include Marlon Brando, Al Pacino, Robert De Niro, Ellen Burstyn, James Dean, Maureen Stapleton, Lee Grant, Dustin Hoffman, Marilyn Monroe, and Paul Newman.

Method Acting emphasizes truth and authenticity, spontaneity, the character's motivation, staying in character, and being exposed to the character's physical environment. Character continuity is important. The character has a back story; he or she does not spring into existence only once the play or movie starts.

Some of the techniques for Method Acting are sort of useful in performing the mental coordinate transformation needed to adopt the mindset of the adversary. I try to mentally prepare and motivate myself and other Vulnerability Assessment team members by encouraging them to invent reasons for hating the client or sponsor, and to desire to humiliate his security program with our discoveries, and create harm and havoc. (I don't mention any of this to the client or sponsor.)

You unlock this door with the key of imagination. Beyond it is another dimension—a dimension of sound, a dimension of sight, a dimension of mind. You're moving into a land of both shadow and substance, of things and ideas. You've just crossed over into the Twilight Zone.
    -- Rod Serling (1924-1975), Introduction to the *Twilight Zone* TV show

---

(Certainly, one does not need to invoke some of the more extreme aspects of Method Acting. It is probably unnecessary, for example, to crawl around on the floor and howl like a wild animal, as some Method Actors were purported to do!)

I also emphasize to myself and VA team members the importance of gleefully looking for problems, rather than trying to reassure ourselves that everything is fine. We need to be like such professional, skeptical fault finders as movie critics, detectives, inspectors, scientific peer reviewers, bloggers, stand-up comedians, and mothers-in-law.

Brainstorming

A key element of any kind of creative exercise like VAs is **brainstorming**. This is cranking out innovative ideas by turning the brain loose. Brainstorming is often where creative ideas are given birth. Unhappily, we've all been in "brainstorming" sessions where any idea that is offered is immediately shot down by colleagues or an overbearing authority figure running the meeting. That is not brainstorming., and it certainly does not engender creative ideas and solutions.

There is evidence that brainstorming sometimes works better with nominal groups—pooled results from individual brainstormers—than with actual ones.
-- Raymond S. Nickerson

One critical fact about creativity is that it is what an individual does, not a group. A brainstorming group can help identify key issues, refine the problem(s), motivate/energize individual members to find creative discoveries, and let ideas feed off each other. But the creativity needs to be done informally, by individuals working primarily outside the group setting.

Could Hamlet have been written by committee, or the Mona Lisa painted by a club? Could the New Testament have been composed as a conference report? Creative ideas don't spring from groups. They spring from individuals.
-- Alfred Whitney Griswold (1885-1959)

Given that good security and good VAs require imagination and creativity, and that neither is the forte of groups or of plodding/linear thinkers, is should not be surprising that security run by bureaucrats and committees is usually deeply flawed and not very innovative or proactive.

If you are going to use a group as part of the brainstorming process, keep it small. Exclude authority figures because they may suppress freewheeling. Creativity experts generally recommend that the ideal group for brainstorming be diverse with enthusiasm for individual differences and eccentricities. The group should be cohesive but not too cohesive, high-energy, and receptive to humor, joy, and fun. Ideally, there would be some friendly and respectful competition between group members. Some sense of urgency is good, but the environment must not be stressful. Interestingly, people who are slightly tired tend to be more creative because this somehow lowers inhibition. Having a "retreat", that is, going to some new location for the group meetings also seems to be beneficial. Not only can it provide a fresh setting, but if travel is involved, it may allow participants to be somewhat tired.

The people who fear humor, and they are many, are suspicious of its power to present things in unexpected lights, to question received opinions, and to suggest unforeseen possibilities.

-- Robertson Davies (1913-1995)

One of the best models for group brainstorming that exhibit many of the above attributes is comedy writing. For a really fun and interesting book about this, read *Caesar's Hours: My Life In Comedy, With Love and Laughter,* by Sid Caesar.

An extremely important concept to keep in mind when brainstorming about vulnerabilities, attacks, or countermeasures is that early on, there must be no attempt to edit, reject, or evaluate ideas. Every idea, no matter how wacky or apparently stupid, gets treated is a gem and and is written down. Discussions of practicality come much later in the VA process. Quantity early on will eventually breed quality.

Nothing can inhibit and stifle the creative process more—and on this there is unanimous agreement among all creative individuals and investigators of creativity—than critical judgment applied to the emerging idea at the beginning stages of the creative process. ... More ideas have been prematurely rejected by a stringent evaluative attitude than would be warranted by any inherent weakness or absurdity in them. The longer one can linger with the idea with judgment held in abeyance, the better the chances all its details and ramifications [can emerge].
-- Eugene Raudsepp (1923-1995)

During the brainstorming phase of a VA, completely insane ideas about how to attack security or about countermeasures involving space aliens, flying monkeys, scuba divers, Elvis impersonators, etc. are very welcome. In my experience, it is remarkable how often crazy ideas can be massaged into something useful if the crazy ideas are simply allowed to organically morph, evolve, and ripen. Moreover, nutty ideas give the brain permission to explore.

There are numerous tips for effective brainstorming in general which also seem to work for VAs. You might want to determine if there is a location or time when you are particularly creative. Many people find taking a shower, or going on a walk, or doing other light exercise helps new ideas to pop into your head. New ideas often appear when you are relaxed and not focusing on the problem—when you least expect it. Surprisingly, recent research suggests that playing music actually inhibits creativity!

We all know your idea is crazy. The question is, is it crazy enough?
-- Niels Bohr (1885-1962)

*Sanity is a one trick pony—all you have is rational thought.
But when you're good and loony, the sky's the limit!*
-- The Tick

Other Tips for Creative Thinking During VAs

* It turns out to be very important to credit specific individuals (not the group!) with the new ideas they come up with. Thus, if Susan comes up with an interesting new attack, it gets known as "Susan's Attack". If Josh proposes a change to the attack, it is "Josh's modification to Susan's Attack".

* Plan and prepare for the fact that the best ideas often come late in the VA process, maybe even when you are writing the final VA Report (or just after you submitted it).

* Be skeptical! Pay close attention to explicit or unstated assumptions, and to security or design features that are widely praised or admired. These are often the source of serious vulnerabilities because there has been insufficient critical, skeptical analysis of them.

> *Nothing is like it seems, but everything is exactly like it is.*
> -- Yogi Berra (1925-2015)

---

* You may want to take an especially close look at the 2nd or 3rd best attacks or countermeasures. You might well be overlooking something that would make them the best solutions.

* With all ideas: elaborate, expand, modify, subvert, exaggerate, and combine with other ideas.

* Pursue hunches and intuition.

* Pursue what is interesting, controversial, contrarian, exciting, or silly.

* If there is widespread agreement about a vulnerability, attack, or countermeasure, re-examine. There may be groupthink taking place, joint false assumptions, or else something important may have been overlooked.

* Develop and explore models, metaphors, and analogies. These can be powerful.

* Ridicule existing security measures and strategies. This frees up the mind and people will be less intimidated by them. Humor in general is good for creativity.

> *To crack a serious problem, crack a joke.*
> -- Haresh Sippy

* Terminology constrains our thinking. Rename everything in your own (and/or silly) words, and think about them in light of the new terminology. Consider different verbs for what the bad guys might want to accomplish: attack, steal, smash, demolish, embarrass, tag, terminate, uncover, purify, spoil, whistleblow, kill, poison, cleanse, etc. Terminology *does* affect our thinking!

> *I cannot imagine any condition which could cause this ship to flounder.*
> *I cannot conceive of any vital disaster happening to this vessel.*
> -- E.J. Smith, Captain of the Titanic, 1912

Chapter 5 Discussion and Thought Questions

1. When, where, and under what conditions are you the most creative? What tricks do you use to come up with innovative solutions to problems or to discover new connections or discoveries?

2. Is your organization tolerant, discouraging, or encouraging of innovative thinking?

3. How do you spot creative people and creative talent?

4. Think about the best and worst brainstorming sessions you have attended for any purpose. What worked well and what did not?

5. Why do you think that groups, even brainstorming groups, tend to suppress creativity and innovation?

6. Why do crazy ideas, humor, and ridicule free up the brain to be innovative?

7. Is creativity an innate ability, or can it be learned and improved? Why?

8. What are some of the reasons that security professionals are often not very creative? Often lack critical thinking skills?

9. Why are models, metaphors, and analogies so useful for getting fresh insights into challenging problems?

10. Do you think being skeptical is a useful mindset for being creative, why or why not? Is cynicism going too far, or is it a useful tool for (a) creativity in general and (b) Vulnerability Assessment in particular?

11. Many Vulnerability Assessors are cynical about the security they see. Do you think this is an occupational hazard of seeing so much flawed security and dumb organizational behavior, or is cynicism a useful tool to do Vulnerability Assessments? Or is it both? Why?

Chapter 6. The VA Report

Never solve a problem for someone, instead, help them figure out how to solve it on their own. Otherwise, you destroy their adaptive competence.
-- Lord Robin

Security managers are sometimes surprised that the VA Report contains not just information about vulnerabilities and attacks, but also recommendations for countermeasures, including design changes or improved use protocols. They view this as more in their purview than for the VAers.

There are, in fact, several reasons why the VA Report must include proposed countermeasures, whether they are ever implemented or not. The VAers have an important perspective on security problems, so their recommendations are worth considering. Even more importantly, a VA Report that is full of nothing but problems and criticisms but no proposed solutions is not going to be well received, and this makes it unlikely that necessary changes will be implemented. Even if security managers ultimate develop their own countermeasures to the problems found in the VA, the recommendations in the VA Report may serve as the nucleus for critical local thinking about those changes.

In fact, there may indeed be more effective, cheaper, or more practical solutions that take into account local conditions, personnel, and resource limitations that the VAers didn't fully appreciate. Also, the recipients of the VA report may conclude (rightly or wrongly) that certain risks are worth taking. They believe that some or all of the security flaws pointed out in the report may be worth knowing, but don't need to be immediately fixed. Indeed, a good VA Report will offer far more suggested countermeasures and recommended design and use protocol changes than are likely to ever be implemented.

A VA can sometimes open the eyes of the sponsor or client (or at least some of their employees) so that they can begin finding their own vulnerabilities, attack scenarios, countermeasures, and improved use protocols. Somehow, seeing a skeptical, imaginative analysis of security involving critical thinking seems to give people permission to begin thinking that way about their own security. In my experience, the low level people in the organization often catch on quicker than their managers or supervisors.

Proposed countermeasures and modifications to the design or use protocols outlined in the VA Report should always rank proposed changes by likely importance, effectiveness, invasiveness, and cost. Some proposed changes will have a bigger potential impact on improving security than others. Many will be surprisingly easy and inexpensive to implement, while others will not.

It is very important that the VA Report open with robust praise for the good aspects of the security under review. There are two purposes for this. We want to encourage the good features and practices to continue. Sometimes they are just accidents! Secondly, we want to set up the reader so that she is more psychologically prepared to hear about the problems.

For a similar reason, it is important early on in the Report to emphasize the severe challenges that the security presents. Higher-ups in organizations who are not security managers, and even some security managers, are often unaware of just how difficult it is to have good security—so, of course, problems are to be expected. Security is never a slam dunk!

The VA Report should also include the following information:

+ identity and experience of the assessors
+ any real or perceived conflicts of interest
+ the time, funds, and resources used
+ any *a priori* constraints or limitations on the scope of the study

- descriptions, photographs, and any video documentation of vulnerabilities, attacks, possible countermeasures, and recommended changes to the design or use protocols
- documentation and specifications (and samples where appropriate) for any materials, tools, electronics, and equipment used in the VA
- documentation and specifications (and samples where appropriate) for any custom tools, electronics, hardware, or software developed for the attacks
- the estimated time, skills, expertise, practice, and resources required by an adversary to execute each attack
- recommendations for resiliency and recovery after attacks

Most VA Reports will also benefit from an Executive Summary at the top, plus a non-sensitive, statistical summary of the findings if the sponsor or client wishes to take public credit for having a VA.

Finally, the VA Report should be delivered to the highest appropriate level without editing, interpretation, or censorship by security employees, supervisors, or middle managers.

Once we know our weaknesses they cease to do us any harm.
-- Georg C. Lichtenberg (1742-1799)

Chapter 6 Discussion and Thought Questions

1. Why is it important for the Vulnerability Assessment Report to open with praise for the current security, and a discussion of how difficult the security challenge really is?

2. Why is there a risk of the findings and recommendations in the VA Report getting lost, hidden, censored, or diluted before they reach the level in the organization that may be able to act on it? Why would some middle man/woman want to interfere?

3. Why could a redacted, non-sensitive summary of the VA report that avoids discussing sensitive security information be of use to the organization, its customers and stakeholders? What should be in that sanitized summary?

4. How should the VA report or security managers go about prioritizing vulnerabilities, attack scenarios, and countermeasures so that the most urgent, effective, and easiest/cheapest to implement are given greatest priority? What factors go into these decisions? How does one choose between urgency, effectiveness, and ease/cheapness? For example, should a security change that costs $1 and has some value for improving security be given a higher priority than a potential change that is substantially more effective but costs many thousands of dollars and is a hassle to implement?

5. Why would some sponsors or clients of a VA be hesitant to let there be a formal written VA Report? Why is this bad Security Culture?

6. Is it ok to have known security vulnerabilities that aren't fixed or mitigated? Why or why not?

Chapter 7. Cognitive Dissonance & Intellectual Humility

You cannot fix a problem that you refuse to acknowledge.
-- Margaret Heffernan

The truth? You can't handle the truth!
-- From Jack Nicholson's testimony
in the movie, *A Few Good Men* (1992)

Vulnerability Assessors often must confront cognitive dissonance in the security that they examine. **Cognitive Dissonance** is the mental tension between what we want to be true (e.g., that we have good security) and what is likely to be true (we don't). It can also be the mental tension that arises when an opinion, attitude, belief, statement, decision, or action we chose in the past is now under challenge by new facts, ideas, beliefs, or people.

Cognitive dissonance itself is not harmful; it is, in fact, more or less unavoidable. The danger comes in not recognizing or in mismanaging cognitive dissonance—something that is common in all human endeavors, not just security. Unrecognized or mishandled cognitive dissonance can lead to self-justification (self-serving rationalization and excuse making), paralysis and stagnation (not addressing problems), confirmation bias and motivated reasoning (interpreting facts and data only in ways that make us feel good), sunk-cost bias (insisting on continuing failed projects or programs because substantial effort and funds have already been spent), excessive fear and anger, and a lot of "shooting the messenger" types of behaviors.

---

*I don't want any yes-men around me. I want everybody
to tell me the truth even if it costs them their job.*
-- Samuel Goldwyn (1912-2007)

Cognitive dissonance shows up in the difference between threats and vulnerabilities. Whereas few security programs claim to face zero threats, many deny (or want to deny) that they have significant vulnerabilities.

Sometimes when I close my eyes, I can't see.
-- Anonymous

Countermeasures to Cognitive Dissonance

So how do we counter cognitive dissonance in security, or more properly, how do we minimize the bad handling of cognitive dissonance? A lot of the potential countermeasures that I have proposed are largely unstudied, but probably make a lot of sense.

One powerful tool is humor. Humor often makes us loosen up and not take ourselves so seriously. What is even more important is that a lot of humor (though not all) is based on the element of surprise. The old (not especially hilarious) joke about why the chicken crossed the road is the archetype. We are surprised and (theoretically) amused at our surprise when we learn that the explanation is not some profound analysis of the chicken's motivation, but rather the vacuous statement that the chicken merely wanted to reach the other side of the road. Being surprised that our expectations were wrong is a reminder that everything we assume or think that we know is not necessarily so. (Isn't it interesting that humor is good for creativity <u>and</u> countering cognitive dissonance?)

I dream of a better tomorrow, where chickens can cross the road and not be questioned about their motives.
-- Ralph Waldo Emerson (1803-1882)

Other tools for overcoming the dangers of cognitive dissonance are about avoiding groupthink. Creativity and diversity of thought should be nurtured, as should differing views or even controversy about security (within limits.) New research suggests that military units are more effective and make better decisions if there is a degree of disagreement about major issues. This may be because disagreements help to reduce groupthink. It may also be because group members have to actually think through and justify their positions to other group members, resulting in more critical thinking and ultimately better decisions.

Security managers should thus seek input from other people, welcome questions and criticism from any quarter, and watch out for over-confidence in themselves and by others. They should become a devil's advocate or, even better, appoint a devil's advocate who intelligently challenges everything.

If everybody is thinking alike, then nobody is thinking.
-- George S. Patton (1885-1945)

It is especially important with security to avoid binary thinking, and to be fully cognizant of just how difficult security really is. The bad guys have most of the advantages. To deal with the inevitable cognitive dissonance, security managers should get comfortable with uncertainty and with being afraid and uncomfortable. That is the nature of dealing with risk. They should educate subordinates on the hazards of cognitive dissonance. They need to have plans for when security fails. This is both for purposes of resiliency and recovery, but also to remind themselves that security *is* going to fail.

Success comes not from having certainty, but being able to live with uncertainty.
-- Jeffrey Fry

Intellectual Humility

Intellectual Humility is a mindset that leaves open the possibility that you may be wrong or misinformed, and that other people may be right, or at least have valuable insights, experience, and knowledge worth listening to. A person who in intellectually humble is not threatened when her ideas are challenged, and is open to discovering personal weaknesses and blind spots. This requires a certain intrinsic curiosity and flexibility of thought. No belief or viewpoint is ever permanently frozen in place.

When you are certain you cannot be fooled, you become easy to fool.
-- Edward Teller (1908-2003)

Especially with security, we need intellectual humility—to not be so sure of what we know. This leaves us open to discovering vulnerabilities and considering changes and improvements in security. Intellectual Humility is also a powerful tool for critical thinking, which is so important for good security and good VAs.

One of the things that makes intellectual humility hard is the Dunning-Kruger Effect: when you lack knowledge or expertise about a subject, you don't know that you lack it. Dunning-Kruger is not denial, it is just ignorance. It is one of the reasons that security managers may be uninterested in learning about their security vulnerabilities.

Probably the best ways to become intellectually humble is to work on keeping an open mind, admit to yourself and others your ignorance and limitations, focus on overall personal growth, mimic someone you know who is intellectually humble, and long for truth rather than for being right.

It ain't what you don't know that gets you into trouble.
It's what you know for sure that just ain't so.
-- Mark Twain (1835-1910)

Perceptual Blindness and Change Blindness

For decades, psychologists have shown repeatedly that people are remarkably poor observers. They see what they expect to see, not what is really there. This is a type of cognitive dissonance.

Even worse, people don't begin to realize just how bad they are at observation, or remembering what they saw. This is exploited all the time by magicians, lawyers, con men, and adversaries. (For a demonstration of the problem, see the Discussion and Thought Questions at the end of the chapter.)

For frontline security personnel, **Perceptual Blindness** (a.k.a. Inattentional Blindness) and **Change Blindness** are major problems. Perceptual Blindness is where you miss things right in front of your eyes because you weren't expecting them and/or are busy mentally processing or monitoring something else. Change Blindness is when you miss noticing changes because your brain has filed away part or all of the scene as being static, and you resist revising that judgement—another kind of cognitive dissonance. These are serious vulnerabilities for such tasks as checking security badges or documents, monitoring live video surveillance, manning gates, going on security rounds, checking for financial irregularities, inspecting tamper-indicating seals, and operating nuclear safeguards equipment.

Possible countermeasures to Perceptual Blindness and Change Blindness include educating frontline security personnel to their existence, demonstrating to them their own poor observation skills using psychologists, videos, and magicians with their sleight-of-hand tricks, training in observational skills, and testing observational skills while they are on duty by introducing anomalous events.

There are other possible countermeasures as well. We can choose people who happen to be relatively good at making reliable observations for security and auditing jobs that require this. We might also be able to rely more on technology to help minimize the need for accurate human observation, or to improve it.

In the case of security guards or inspectors monitoring a complex or chaotic scene, it may be useful (when possible) to choose one or more security guards or inspectors to be the generalist(s). They examine the overall scene without specific assigned detailed observational responsibilities. They focus on the unexpected and the rare, rather than getting preoccupied with the routine. This approach might be helpful for security guards who monitor a secure access point while also having to deal with distracting visitors or the public. It might also be useful for international nuclear safeguards inspectors who are often rushed, stressed, and jet lagged.

Ring the bells that still can ring.
Forget your perfect offering.
There is a crack in everything.
That's how the light gets in.
-- The song *Anthem*, by Leonard Cohen (1934-2016)

Chapter 7 Discussion and Thought Questions

1. If you doubt your own ineptitude at observation, watch the whodunnit video on the Internet produced by the Lord Mayer of London to encourage bicycle safety: https://www.youtube.com/watch?v=ubNF9QNEQLA. Better yet, show it to someone without telling them to pay close attention, and observe their reaction. (Bad guys rarely advertise when it is time to pay extra special attention.)

2. Why do you think people are such bad observers? What are some of the biological survival benefits of not over-analyzing every scene?

3. What other countermeasures can you think of for Perceptual/Inattentional Blindness and Change Blindness? Are some people likely to be better observers than others and why would this be? Do you think we can learn to be better observers?

4. What are some examples from your past where cognitive dissonance in you or others has caused problems both for security and for other things?

5. What countermeasures to cognitive dissonance do you use? What other countermeasures can you think of that might also work, or that you've seen other people using?

6. Why is not wanting to hear bad news an example of poor handling of cognitive dissonance?

7. Does the CEO of your organization have a problem with cognitive dissonance? Does your boss?

8. Why do you think people hate being wrong so much? Why do they hate it even when there aren't any witnesses?

9. Does your group or organization have a devil's advocate? If so, is that person appreciated?

10. If you were tasked with hiring a security manager, how could you determine if she is likely to have problems in properly dealing with cognitive dissonance?

Chapter 8. Sham Rigor & The Fear of VAs

You can buy muscles, but you can't buy cojones.
-- Bas Rutten

Subjectivity and Uncertainty

Psychologists have long known that human beings crave "cognitive closure", i.e., a definitive, unassailable solution to problems. Ambiguity and uncertainty are scary, especially for important issues like security. The fact of the matter is, however, that ambiguity, uncertainty, and having differing views about security is not a weaknesses. Rather, it is a sign of realism, intellectual humility, and a healthy Security Culture. To think otherwise is to buy into sham rigor.

The notion of a cold, analytic, actuarial risk assessment is largely a myth. Risk is a social construct that incorporates value judgments about context and cause.
-- Henry Willis

In my experience, many bureaucrats and engineers (who unfortunately often run security programs) have a horror of any controversy or uncertainty about how to do security. This is absurd. Anything as complicated and challenging as security that involves making so many difficult value judgements and tradeoffs, doing prognostication, analyzing complicated metrics, undertaking tricky optimizations of resources, managing people, predicting malicious behavior, taking on motivated adversaries, and utilizing a mix of hard and soft sciences is going to result in uncertainty and differing views on how to proceed. A diversity of viewpoints about security is not a bug, it's a feature!

The reality is that there is no guaranteed or rigorous way to do security, or to be certain that we have enough of it. Any claim to the contrary is not just sham rigor, it is foolish and dangerous. Indeed, sham rigor is found nearly everywhere in security, in inept and arrogant security programs, security products with little or no security built in, astonishing security hype and snake oil, and weak security assessment methods.

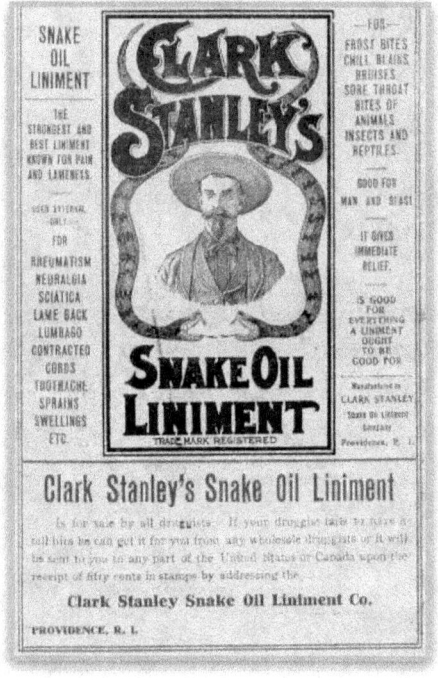

Due to the rapid changes in the complexity of both technology and organizations over the past two decades, historical data has become less significant. Risk measurement and the identification of consequences require a combination of experience, skills, imagination, and creativity. This emphasis on subjective measurements is borne out in practice.

-- David McNamee

Vulnerabilities, attack scenarios, and countermeasures are best found through creative thinking, not via some imaginary, automated or rigorous formula or model. This is especially true because there is a remarkable dearth of sophisticated research into physical security and best practices. Cyber security is substantially better in this regard but still often falls short. This lack of security R&D in both the technical and social sciences limits having rigorous research- and evidence-based security practice.

People generally prefer the predictable. Few recognize how destructive this can be, how it imposes severe limits on variability and thus makes whole populations fatally vulnerable to the shocking ways our universe can throw the dice.

-- Frank Herbert (1920-1986)

Security engineers and bureaucrats tend to fear subjective methods for analyzing security. By their nature, creative VAs and effective Risk Management approaches are ultimately subjective. The process is rarely consistent, predictable, or fully quantifiable. This is in contrast to the more consistent and ostensibly objective—but less effective—security analysis methods discussed in Chapter 1 such as TAs and security surveys.

So why are the best VAs ultimately subjective? There are a number of reasons. Frequently, discovered vulnerabilities are not just a shock to developers, manufacturers, vendors, end-users, and security managers, they are often a shock to the Vulnerability Assessors! So predictability cannot be expected. The best ideas about vulnerabilities, attacks, and countermeasures are often clever and creative, and seem to pop up "out of nowhere" (and late), like creative ideas do in other fields. And then again, whenever my VAers looked at the same security device, system, or program a 2nd or 3rd time, we usually found new vulnerabilities that we and other vulnerability assessors missed. Moreover, I would claim that nobody really understands security or VAs very well, so the subjective nature of good VAs is probably not particularly surprising. Another factor is that effective VAs are proactive and predictive, and that is difficult to formalize.

Objections to NORQ VAs

There seem to be 5 main objections that organizations and security managers often raise about creative, NORQ VAs. NORQ stands for **N**on-**O**bjective, non-**R**eproducible, and non-**Q**uantitative. While these objections are understandable, they lack any real merit.

Objection 1: Critical security applications are too important to be left to "flaky" creative analysis. Counter Argument: Critical security applications are too important <u>not</u> to utilize all the tools available to us, especially powerful (though admittedly unpredictable) tools like creative, NORQ analysis methods

Objection 2: Right brain thinking won't yield the "right" answer. Counter Argument: There usually is no one "right" answer. Security is a very difficult optimization problem involving many complex trade-offs and value judgments, and it usually has problematic metrics. Even if there were one "right" answer for security, there is no way to prove it is the "right" answer. We need instead to focus on getting a good answer. NORQ analysis can help us with that.

Objection 3: Right brain thinking will lead to disagreements and controversies. Counter Argument: That is one of the strengths of NORQ security analysis, not a weakness! Anything as important and difficult as security, with all its complex unknowns, trade-offs, human factors, management challenges, and value judgments, is not just likely to be controversial, it <u>should</u> be controversial.

Objection 4: If I can't reproduce the results of our security analysis, they are of no use. Counter Argument: Perhaps someday we will understand security and creative analysis well enough to be able to provide both effective and reproducible results. In the meantime, it is irresponsible not to take advantage of NORQ analysis (in conjunction with ORQ analysis) to help us improve security, even if creative NORQ methods are uneven.

Objection 5: All the vulnerabilities won't be found with NORQ analysis. Counter Argument: ORQ techniques won't find all the vulnerabilities, either, and are usually worse at it than NORQ methods. More to the point, it is not even possible to find all the vulnerabilities for a non-trivial security device, system, or program, no matter what techniques we use. Even if we could somehow find them all, it isn't possible to prove that we have done so.

Countermeasures to Fear

One thing that can help with the irrational fear associated with the idea of creative NORQ VAs is to remind security managers that their security task is challenging, and that numerous vulnerabilities are absolutely inevitable. It should also be pointed out that it is not necessary to totally eliminate every discovered vulnerability, or counter every possible attack. For example, it is probably impractical to try to eliminate the risk of a terrorist crashing an airplane into your factory. You probably won't, for example, be allowed to place anti-aircraft guns on the roof of the facility and open fire on suspicious aircraft. You can, however, possibly design the facility to minimize damage and loss of life should such an attack take place, and plan ahead for rapid recovery.

Fear is a reaction you have when you are getting closer to the truth.
-- Jim Palmer

If discovered vulnerabilities and attacks are not mitigated, this must, of course, be decided on the basis of sound Risk Management, not cognitive dissonance.

Security managers need to be reminded that the recommendations arising from the VA are just that—recommendations—and not mandates. They should also be advised that just because the best VAs are NORQ in character, this is not to say that quantitative, reproducible, formalistic, and objective techniques for analyzing security have no place in improving security. It's just that they cannot be the only techniques employed.

If you look for truth, you may find comfort in the end; if you look for comfort you will get neither truth nor comfort…only soft soap and wishful thinking to begin, and in the end, despair.
-- C.S. Lewis (1898-1963)

Security Standards, Guidelines, and Regulations

Security standards, guidelines, and regulations are often thought of by security managers and organizations as the gold standard for security. While they are sometimes useful as thought triggers, many, in my view, are either deeply flawed or even harmful. They tend to be too general, overly simplified, and/or written with the wrong security mindset using appallingly bad terminology and sloppy reasoning. Special interests often have far too much influence in developing them. Not everyone involved in developing a security standard or guideline actually knows what they are talking about, or has the best of overall intentions.

The one-size-fits all nature of most security standards, guidelines, and regulations are unhelpful. Local conditions need to be considered to get optimal security. Security standards, guidelines, and regulations are often used to veto improvements in security, and to shut down critical thinking or questioning. I've seen that frequently in the federal government.

Another big problem is that many organizations use their compliance with one security standards as "proof" that they have good overall security, even when the standard only covers limited aspects of enterprise security. This can impede necessary security improvements. It is common, for example, for companies to maintain they have excellent cyber security because they comply with the Payment Card Industry Data Security (PCI) Standard. This standard, however, is about how to handle credit card information, it is not really about cyber security in any comprehensive sense. Another example is when security manufacturers claim strong security for their products because they meet UL or ISO standards. Often those standards are about safety or quality control, not security. Even when such standards cover certain aspects of security, they are not the definitive word on all aspects of product security.

Another problematic "gold standard" for security is "best practice". While there is often a remarkable degree of agreement among security experts as to what constitutes best practice, it is not rigorously defined or measured.

There are, however, two advantages of the idea of best practice. Firstly, "best practice" often actually *is* better than what takes place in most security programs. Secondly, the idea that there may be better ways of doing things is a healthy mindset.

> *Definition—Best Practice: Those guys don't know what the hell they are doing, either, but at least they seem confident.*
> *-- Devil's Dictionary of Security Terms*

Chapter 8 Discussion and Thought Questions

1. What examples of sham rigor are you aware of in security?

2. What examples of lousy or over-hyped security products or services are you aware of? What makes them so bad? Why are they so misrepresented?

3. Can you think of other ways to lessen the fear of organizations and security managers about creative VAs?

4. Why can't creative, inventive thinking in general be formalized and made rigorous? How about the creative VA process?

5. How can you decide if a security standard, guideline, or regulation has merit for your security?

6. What security "best practices" are you aware of? Do you think they truly are the best way to do security, why or why not?

Chapter 9. Security Culture & Security Theater

Sometimes security implementations look fool proof.
And by that I mean proof that fools exist.
-- Dan Philpot

Security Culture can be defined as an organization's security policies, practices, priorities, norms, behaviors, beliefs, attitudes, perceptions, and mindset. Sometimes the more informal aspects of Security Culture such as perceptions, beliefs, and "water cooler talk" are instead considered part of **Security Climate**. This, however, is a term that is more common among scholars than security practitioners.

There is widespread recognition that an organization's security will be no better than its Security Culture. There is also some general recognition that informal (Security Climate) aspects of an organization are even more important than the formal ones. There is less understanding of how to measure and engender a healthy Security Culture.

> "I don't have the first clue who he is talking about because all I worry about is Jerome."
> -- Basketball player Jerome James, responding
> to criticism from his coach that he was selfish

What is a Good Security Culture?

It is clear that a good Security Culture has certain essential attributes. In a healthy Security Culture, insiders in the organization are motivated to follow good security practices, are focused on doing so, and encourage their coworkers to do the same. Security and security thought are organically integrated into all the organizations activities. There is a lively, ongoing discussion and even conflicting views about security and how to optimally do it.

In a good Security Culture, the old paradigm about who does security is replaced with a new paradigm. Under the old paradigm, trained security personnel provide security. Security managers are the main experts on security, while regular employees, contractors, and visitors are the enemies of good security. Under the new paradigm—the insider threat not withstanding—regular employees, contractors, visitors, local authorities, vendors, and neighbors provide security, while security professionals provide help and advice. Regular employees are the main experts on local security.

Another old paradigm that is rejected in a good Security Culture is the idea that security is painful, will be resisted by employees, and must inconvenience and hassle employees, contractors, and visitors in order to be effective. Indeed, the degree of hassling often becomes a (deeply flawed) metric for security. Under the new paradigm adopted by a good Security Culture, security must not interfere with productivity or morale any more than absolutely necessary. This is important because once security becomes the enemy of productivity and of employees, all is lost. Under this new paradigm, employee acceptance is one metric for effective security, not the degree of employee misery.

VAers need to check if there is special treatment for VIPs—do they get to bypass usual security procedures? This sends entirely the wrong message that security is only for grunts. Also, security professionals need to be approachable helpers who are

sympathetic to employees and local conditions. They should not be thugs and secret police there to trip up employees.

Security Theater

Poor Security Cultures often have a lot of Security Theater. **Security Theater** is sham or ceremonial security. It ostensibly involves protecting people and other assets, but actually has little or nothing to do with countering adversaries.

The best way to spot Security Theater is with an effective VA. There are, however, characteristics that strongly suggest the presence of Security Theater even without bothering with a full-blown VA.

Security Theater will often be present when there is a very challenging security problem, and a sense of extreme urgency for dealing with it. (There were, for example, many ridiculous "security measures" that were implemented immediately after the 9/11 attack.) Security Theater often involves deploying fad or pet technologies that have not been rigorously evaluated or carefully thought through. The seemingly "magic" security device, technology, strategy, or program will have lots of "feel good" aspects to it. In reality, however, true security does not usually leave people feeling comfortable.

You can be fairly certain that you are looking at Security Theater if questions, concerns, or dissent are not welcome or tolerated, and if there is the presence of strong emotion, hype, over confidence, arrogance, ego, and/or pride.

As if there were safety in stupidity alone.
-- Henry David Thoreau (1817-1862)

***

Signs of likely Security Theater:
- conflicts of interest
- fad or pet technologies
- rigged "demos" and "tests"
- lots of rules only the good guys follow
- critics and questioners are angrily attacked
- questions/concerns are not welcome or tolerated
- "feel good" aspects when it is a difficult security problem
- no independent review, devil's advocates, or effective VAs
- excess of ego, pride, fear, over-confidence, or arrogance
- adversaries, attacks, procedures, and use protocols are poorly defined
- bureaucrats, committees, or people who don't get security are in charge

***

Security Theater will also be strongly implicated if there are major conflicts of interest, including when the developers or promoters of the technologies or concepts are the deciders, implementers, or "testers". Also, Security Theater is likely if there is no well-defined adversary, no well-defined use protocol(s), and no effective VAs. Be extremely wary if the technical people involved are mostly engineers, and if the people in charge know little about either security or the technology. An intense desire to "save the world" is always admirable, but it often leads to wishful thinking—a big problem with nuclear security/safeguards and homeland security, in my view.

I was born to make mistakes, not to fake perfection.
-- rapper Drake

Compliance-Based Security Versus Real Security

"Compliance-Based Security" is an oxymoron. We don't get good security by demanding that employees mindlessly follow security rules established by clueless bureaucrats. We get good security by establishing a good Security Culture, avoiding Security Theater, factoring in human behavior and organizational characteristics, and motivating and empowering employees to make good security happen.

Security managers and organizations that base their security largely on rule compliance are confusing Control with Security. This is a common blunder.

Adherence to security rules, policies, procedures, and regulations—while often necessary—is no guarantee of good security. In fact, rigid, mindless compliance and good security are often wholly incompatible.

As a general rule of thumb, I have found that at least 30% of the security rules in large organizations actually make security worse! This can occur when the security rules, regulations, laws, policies, standards, and guidelines are imposed by high-level bureaucrats in a one-size-fits-all manner, with few (if any) sanity checks at the local level.

If nothing else, ill-conceived or ill-fitting security rules may be little more than Security Theater. At the very least, they may draw valuable time, energy, and attention away from real security efforts. All the paperwork, bureaucracy, data recording, and preparation for audits may simply become distractions. Even worst, they send the message that Security = Busy Work, and that the brass are responsible for security, not me. It makes security an "us versus them" kind of thing.

Lame rules can create harmful cynicism about security among security and non-security employees, which leads to a weak Security Culture. Even worse, the auditors may become the enemy in the mind of employees, not the bad guys. (See Chapter 11 for how effective security awareness training can help improve Security Culture.)

Another problem with Compliance-Based Security is that it often involves granting access to numerous auditors, overseers, micro-managers, and checkers of the checkers. This can substantially increase the insider threat.

I've seen and heard of many specific examples of Compliance harming Security. A common and particularly disturbing example of compliance hurting security is when doing only the minimum required by the compliance requirements results in security that is not good enough. Carried to an extreme—which I have personally witnessed multiple times—it means that the minimum specified by the compliance rules constrains what is allowed. We won't be allowed to make a significant security improvement not actually required by the auditors. For example, federal requirements for anti-malware on SCADA control systems (such as used for power utilities) mandate measures that are weaker than many SCADA security managers would like to implement but the federal rules prohibit a better security solution.

I know of many cases where an organization had to decide between a real security solution and the minimum required by the compliance rules. Guess which one usually wins out?

Other, more concrete and less "cultural" examples of Compliance harming Security include:
- An over-emphasis in the rules and regulations about gates, entry points, and fences (which typically create only a 4.5 to 15 second access delay) leads to failure to consider other attack modes and vulnerabilities, resulting in bad security.

- Overly rigid rules, such as requirements for predictable guard patrols, routes, schedules, and shift changes that make it much easier for attackers to avoid or negate the guard force.

- Rules that only good guys follow, e.g., you must remove your hat and sunglasses in the bank. These waste time and create cynicism about security.

- The federal government has so many different kinds of classifications and security badges among the various agencies that it is difficult to keep them all straight. (The situation has, however, improved somewhat in recent years.)

- Mindlessly banning new technology, rather than trying to intelligently accommodate it. We saw this kind of "cultural lag" (a term coined by William F. Ogburn in 1922) when thumb drives first came out. All this does is to make security the enemy of productivity and employees, engender cynicism about security, and encourage employees to break the rule to get things done—making later rules easier to break.

In thinking about Compliance versus Security, perhaps the following joke is illuminating:

An old married couple were watching the news on television. The weatherman said a snowstorm was coming and that cars should be parked on the odd-numbered side of the street to facilitate snow removal. "Guess I better move the car," said the husband has he rose to put on his jacket.

A few days later, the couple heard on television that another storm was coming and that this time, cars were supposed to be parked on the even-numbered side of the street. The old man got up to move the car.

Two weeks later, the couple was again watching the weather report on television. The weatherman was saying, "another huge blizzard is now bearing down on the city and cars must be parked on the....", when suddenly the power failed and the television went blank. The old man turned to his wife and said, "Now what should we do"? His wife said, "Well, dear, maybe you should just leave the car in the garage tonight."

Transparency Versus Security By Obscurity

It is counter-intuitive, but security is usually better when it is transparent (within obvious limits). Transparency allows for review, analysis, criticism, and multiple viewpoints. It permits better security metrics, quality control, accountability, and employee buy-in. Transparency helps to protect against security over-reach, illegality, unethical conduct, and violations of employee rights and privacy.

Security based on keeping long-terms secrets—so called "Security By Obscurity"—doesn't really work. People, organizations, and insiders simply cannot keep long-term secrets. Whether this is true for your organization or not, it is always necessary to assume the bad guys understand what you are doing in your security. Insiders are always available to provide useful information to adversaries, either inadvertently or deliberately.

There are, of course, short-term secrets that may be worth trying to protect. Things like current computer passwords, the schedule for guard rounds, and exactly when a hazardous shipment will hit the road. These short-term secrets should receive the greatest attention rather than wasting energy on trying to protect fixed, long-term secrets.

When organizations do need to keep secrets, they should limit what they decide to protect to what is truly critical. When everything is highly confidential or classified (including what you had for lunch), then nothing is!

Chapter 9 Discussion and Thought Questions

1. Why is the new paradigm that "employees, contractors, and visitors do security, while security professionals help" better than the old paradigm? Which paradigm is mostly in place in your organization?

2. Why do you think Security Theater is so seductive? Why do people often prefer it to real security?

3. What are some countermeasures to Security Theater?

4. What are some examples of likely Security Theater in your organization?

5. To what extend do you or your organization rely on Security by Obscurity? Compliance-Based Security?

6. How would you make the argument that Compliance is not the best way to get good Security?

7. Is Compliance-Based Safety more or less of a problem than Compliance-Based Security? Why or why not?

8. Most cyber systems get lots of attempted attacks per day. Most physical security is attacked much less frequently. How does this affect how people do and think about cyber security versus physical security?

Chapter 10. Security Metrics, The Fallacy of Precision, and Marginal Analysis

As far as the laws of mathematics refer to reality, they are not certain;
and as far as they are certain, they do not refer to reality.
-- Albert Einstein (1879-1955)

The Fallacy of Precision

Security Metrics are quantitative measurements of certain aspects of security. Generally speaking, we don't really understand things that we do not measure. This does not, however, mean that everything that can be measured is worth measuring, or that it is easy to decide what, how, and when to measure. There is also no guarantee that the security metrics we use are at rigorous, or even relevant.

Security metrics can help VAers to understand a security program. They can also be used by security managers to see if security is improving or degenerating over time. Metrics can be used to justify security expenditures. Security metrics, however, should never be thought of as a means for "assuring" good security.

I don't mean to brag, but I put together a puzzle
in 1 day that said, "2-4 years" on the box.
-- Anonymous

One of the common problems with security metrics is that the are often susceptible to the Fallacy of Precision. This is a big problem in many human endeavors, not just security.

Vulnerability Assessment

There are two types of Fallacy of Precision. Type 1 is confusing precision with accuracy. Type 2 is fake rigor in taking numbers overly seriously that we or others largely made up.

An example of Type 1 Fallacy of Precision is believing that all the digits your calculator spits out have meaning. (Significant figures is a constant struggle with my college students.) Another example is notoriously inaccurate tire gauges. A third Type 1 example is hiring college graduate X instead of Y because X had a college GPA that was 0.001 higher than Y's, even though the two students took very different courses taught by very different professors, and student X majored in Ultimate Frisbee at Beach State University while Y majored in engineering at Stanford.

"Better make it six, I can't eat eight."
-- Baseball player Dan Osinski, when a waitress asked if he wanted his pizza cut into 6 or 8 slices

---

An example of Type 2 Fallacy of Precision includes largely made-up numbers like 90% of all possible points in a course is an "A". (Where did that come from, how does the professor adjust the assessments to fine-tune to that level, and what does an "A" mean, anyway?) Other Type 2 examples are national security threat levels; numeric values to quantify the relative risk from different threats; Pizza, Movie, and Quarterback ratings; and lists of the top 10 baseball players or physicists of all time. These tend to be value judgements that are difficult to make, much less turn into meaningful numbers. Once a number is assigned, however, people tend to place great faith in the rigor of the number because numbers have an aura of definitiveness, even if the process of assigning that number is ambiguous, deeply, flawed, or absurd.

Security Metrics, Fallacy of Precision, and Marginal Analysis

*There's no sense in being precise when you don't
even know what you're talking about.*
-- John von Neumann (1903-1957)

Metrics Mistakes to Avoid

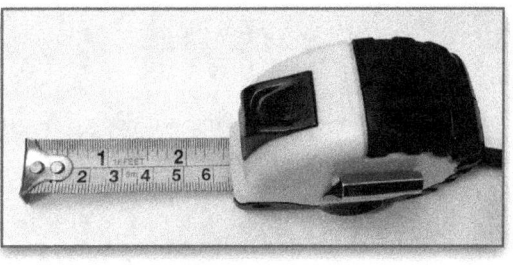

There are a number things that must be avoided with a security metric. It must not be plagued by the Fallacy of Precision, nor should it mostly be about Security Theater (discussed in the previous Chapter). There needs to be recognition that security effectiveness is not measured by how much productive work gets impeded, nor by how much employees get hassled or inconvenienced. Furthermore, security metrics need to measure actual security, not security management activities and busywork. And security metrics should not be used for setting arbitrary thresholds as goals.

It is also essential that we measure the important things, not just the easy things.

Other common problems with security metrics include comparing apples to oranges, getting tripped up by the the Santayana Effect (measuring quantity but not quality), failing to measure aspects of Security Culture, and deploying metrics that drive undesirable employee behaviors. A key mistake is to "teach to the test". This means making employees and security professionals become so obsessed with playing to the metrics that actual security gets ignored. Our goal needs to be good security, not good looking numbers!

The use of non-orthogonal metrics is often a problem. When two security metrics are orthogonal, this means that they measure different things and are not strongly correlated. When two security metrics are non-orthogonal, they may, at least partially, be measuring the same thing but misleadingly counting it twice.

It is difficult to decide how to assign proper weights to various security metrics. Certainly they cannot automatically have the same weights, i.e., be equally important. Unfortunately, this often happens, or else the choice of weighting is mostly arbitrary.

Unconventional Security Metrics

Now we turn to considering a number of rarely used security metrics that might be worth considering for use by VAers and security managers.

- **Degree of security transparency.** Somewhat counter-intuitively, security is usually better when it is transparent because this allows for review, assessment, criticism, questions, improvements, quality control, accountability, and employee buy-in. "Security by Obscurity" is not a viable security strategy. People and organizations simply cannot keep long-term secrets. Moreover, you usually have to assume anyway that adversaries (insiders or outsiders) understand your security. More transparency is generally better, within common-sense limits.

- **Amount of thoughtful pushback.** Pushback against auditors and high-level security rules to allow for local conditions is often a good thing. The key test for local security practice ought to be whether it is good security, not whether it follows the mindless, one-size-fits-all rules mandated by high-level bureaucrats with no understanding of the local environment. Pushback—which is dangerous to employees' careers in many organizations—suggests there has been local critical thinking about security, and that security is being taken seriously. With pushback, more is generally better, within reason.

- **Amount of disagreement about security.** How often are there issues of disagreement or even controversy about how much security to have and how to provide it, by both security professionals in the organization and regular employees? More is generally better, within reason.

- **Disgruntlement mitigation.** What percentage of the time when managers and HR are aware of allegations of an unfair or hostile work environment (bully bosses, coercion, sexual or racial harassment, etc.) do they take positive actions, and don't retaliate against the alleged victims. While disgruntlement is only one of many motivators for inside attacks, it is one of the easiest to counter.

- **Employee turnover rates** for both security and non-security personnel. This is closely related to the insider risk. Rates should be compared averages across that particular industry. Generally, the lower the turnover rate the better, as long as stagnation can be avoided with low turnover rates.

- **Number of employee grievances filed.** How frequently are the organization's grievance complaint process and employee assistance programs used? They will only be used frequently if employees view them as safe, effective, and legitimate. Perception is what is important, not objective reality.

- **Percent of security personnel for whom security is a career choice.** Security Departments that are full of people who don't care if they do security, count pencils, or dish out meatloaf in the cafeteria don't tend to be the most dedicated to security. (Watch out especially for security personnel who moved over from HR!) The higher the percent, the better.

- **Frequency of formal and informal communications between security personnel (including low-level personnel) and non-security employees and contractors.** Security by "walking around" is an effective strategy.

- **Resiliency preparation.** Prevention is difficult. A good security program needs to be ready in advance to lead recovery after a serious security incident, including attacks such as hacking, tampering, and counterfeiting.

- **Amount of "What Ifs?"** How often do employees and security personnel mentally or physically rehearse possible security incidents, and how often are novel incidents considered? Even wildly implausible scenarios get people thinking creatively and critically about security!

- **Frequency of formal and informal vulnerability assessments.** More is usually better, within reason.

- **Number of suggestions for security improvements**, including from low-level personnel and non-security employees.

- **Minor security incidents as predictors.** Do minor security incidents or errors serve as statistical precursors to serious incidents? This is a useful thing to know, as it might help us predict in what teams or departments serious security incidents are most likely to occur.

- **Frequency of sanity checks on security rules.** What is measured is the extent to which there is discussion with, and sanity checks by, employees affected by the security rules. Also, are there periodic sunset reviews of security rules to see if they need to be changed or eliminated? With sanity checks and security rule reviews, more is typically better.

- **Mention of bad guys.** How often do terms like "hackers", "adversaries", "tamperers", "counterfeiters", and "bad guys" appear in oral and written communication inside the organization as a whole? Many organizations discourage or ban such talk. If employees and managers don't talk a lot about the bad guys, how are they going to focus on countering them? As in *Harry Potter*, "he whose name must never be spoken" is a terrible security practice! With this metric, more is better unless we reach the point of paranoia.

- **Other measurements of Security Culture.** These are not measurements of rates of adherence to security rules!

- **Number of security changes recently introduced.** Security is often hampered by cognitive dissonance and inertia. Within reason, the more deliberate changes that are implemented in security the better, especially for large organizations.

Marginal Analysis

This last metric leads us to the idea of "Marginal Analysis". In mathematics and economics, "marginal" means rate of change, or how much output changes with a change in input.

It should be obvious that securing even a medium-sized enterprise or facility is a very complex minimization problem. Risk needs to be minimized while considering thousands of different adjustable security parameters (variables) involving security personnel, chosen technologies, spatial and temporal deployment of resources, possible security strategies, assets to be protected, threats, vulnerabilities, training, dollars spent, etc. This is very much like a classic, mathematical minimization problem in N-dimensional space, where N is quite large.

The figure below shows a 3-dimensional schematic of risk plotted as a function of only 2 security parameters. Thus, for this example, N=3, much simpler than a real security risk minimization problem. Note that the risk surface has multiple peaks and valleys, and is quite complex.

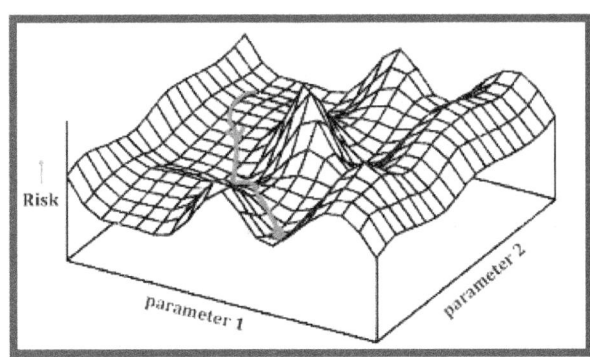

In theory, the goal for a security manger in our over-simplified model is to find the values for the two security parameters at the "location" of the lowest valley in the risk surface; this is the point of minimum risk.

The idea with Marginal Analysis is to introduce changes—real or theoretical—in your security program, and then determine if the risk is lowered as a result. If it is, try additional similar changes to the parameters to see if you can get the risk even lower. If the risk instead increases, try moving in approximately the opposite direction. The goal is to travel "down" the gray path shown in the figure by adjusting the value of various parameters in an attempt to find the minimum of the risk surface, and much more importantly, the values of the various parameters that gives this minimum risk.

We can conclude that we have "pretty good security" if no changes significantly lower the risk because this would mean we are at the bottom of the hills. This method for evaluating the effectiveness of our security may be more practical than a difficult, absolute determination of security effectiveness.

To improve is to change; to be perfect is to change often.
-- Winston Churchill (1874-1965)

Somewhat counter-intuitively, the changes in your security in the actual N-dimensional space should involve variations in more than just 1 parameter at a time. (In this sense, it is not like a scientific experiment.) The changes will usually be minor. Every once in a while, however, it is important to consider large changes. This is because you may currently be in a local valley in the risk surface. There might be a lower valley over the next hill or mountain, and a large change could allow you to locate this lower risk. (It is, however, important not to let the best be the enemy of the good. Often a good security solution is acceptable rather than demanding the absolute best, i.e., the absolute lowest valley in all of N-dimensional risk space.)

Now the risk surface in the figure is constantly morphing and fluctuating over time with changes in threats, assets, personnel, technologies, budgets, etc. So this process of introducing changes to see if the risk gets lowered is ongoing and not a one-time thing.

It is also important to recognize that the mathematical N-dimensional minimization problem is only an analogy. The process is not really mathematical, and you do not need to draw or try to visualize N-dimensional space—which isn't really possible anyway!

We do not yet understand enough about security to do this complete minimization process mathematically in any realistic way. Perhaps someday we will.

In summary, here is the recipe for Marginal Analysis:

1. <u>Continuously</u> try incremental changes (real or theoretic) in your security to see if they improve security, meaning the risk decreases.

2. If the risk decreases, try more change in that "direction" in N-dimensional space. If not, try another direction.

3. Somewhat counter-intuitively, change multiple parameters simultaneously.

4. Occasionally try large changes in an attempt to escape possible local minima in the risk surface.

5. You have "pretty good security" if new changes do not significantly lower the risk.

To try to be better is to be better.
-- Charlotte Saunders Cushman (1816-1876)

An obvious question to ask is, how do you know if a given set of changes improves or degrades your security, i.e., lowers or raises the risk (and takes you "downhill" in N-dimensional space)? There are several possible answers:

Possible Answer 1: It doesn't matter. The main goal of Marginal Analysis is to encourage change, flexibility, and critical thinking about your security. Whether the change is actually implemented or merely contemplated, any reasonable estimate (even if subjective) of whether there is security improvement or not may be adequate. In any event, it is usually easier to judge incremental improvements in security than absolute effectiveness.

Possible Answer 2: For a more nuanced approach, the changes can be implemented for real, then the security system studied for evidence of improvement or degradation using prudent security metrics and observations..

Possible Answer 3: Perhaps the best approach is to let independent vulnerability assessors, threat assessors, risk analysts, subject matter experts, and your own employees and security professionals help you determine whether the change (implemented or contemplated) actually improves your security.

The ultimate question worth considering with Marginal Analysis is the following: Can continually focusing on changes help us be alert, flexible, adaptable, and proactive about security, rather than being stuck with the inertia, reactive approaches, wishful thinking, cognitive dissonance, and groupthink that so often plague security? I don't know the answer, but perhaps Marginal Analysis is worth a try!

Don't give a permanent solution to a temporary situation.
-- Martin Uzochukwu Ugwu

Chapter 10 Discussion and Thought Questions

1. Why are numeric values so seductive when we're dealing with complex matters?

2. What other examples of the Fallacy of Precision (Type 1 and Type 2) have you experienced? Which are Type 1, which are Type 2, and which are both?

3. Which of the proposed unconventional security metrics do you think have merit, and why? What problems do you see with the other proposed metrics?

4. What security metrics do you like, either that you currently use or that you would like to use?

5. Why are disagreements about how much security to have and how to provide it (a) inevitable and (b) actually a good thing (within reason)? When does controversy about security become too much?

6. Do you think Marginal Analysis has some usefulness? Why or why not? What are its potential strengths and weaknesses? Does making a lot of changes in security have value?

7. Is it possible to have too many security changes, occurring too rapidly? How would you determine if this was happening? In what ways could adversaries exploit an organization that makes a lot of security changes over short periods of time?

8. How would you determine in Marginal Analysis if a security change is for the better? Or do you buy the argument that maybe it doesn't matter, that there is merit just in making changes and guesstimating whether there are or are not slight security improvements?

9. Do you think that someday, we will have such a sophisticated understanding of security that we can rigorously and mathematically minimize the risk surface in N-dimensional space, and the results will actually be of practical value? Why or why not?

Chapter 11. Insider Threat Mitigation

We have met the enemy, and he is us.
-- Walt Kelly (1913-1973)

One of the key issues that a Vulnerability Assessor needs to examine is how the organization or security program under study handles the insider threat—the possibility of insiders attacking security, or assisting with attacks. The lack of good mitigation efforts to counter the insider threat is a very serious vulnerability.

An **insider** is someone with special access or knowledge of your organization and its activities, and/or a person who works there (or used to). Insiders can be employees, contractors, craftspeople, service providers, lawyers, consultants, vendors, visitors, and retirees or other ex-employees. Many organizations underestimate the insider risk from low-level employees like custodians, secretaries, and people who restock soda vending machines. Such personnel often have wide access to a facility without attracting much attention.

Background Checks

For many organizations, virtually the only method used to address insider threat is a one-time background check, done at the time of employee hire. Unfortunately, however, employees often start out being loyal and diligent, but things change over time. Disgruntlement or personal problems may set in. This is why background checks—despite their limitations in preventing insider attacks—should be conducted every few years, especially for critical personnel.

Another common problem is that background checks are often done only on employees, while contractors, consultants, vendors and others in key positions are ignored. And when background checks are done, they may be mostly superficial, such as checking driving records for employees whose job won't substantially involve driving, or doing only local criminal history checks. It is also common to give too much weight to temporarily bad credit histories. More profound background checks verify educational credentials, look at any litigation history of the person, are wary of bland job recommendations (which may be covering up serious problems), and include interviews with coworkers, colleagues, family, and neighbors, plus an in-depth interview with the employee. When and where allowed, examination of employees' public social media postings may also provide important insights.

Forbidden things have a secret charm.
-- Pubilus Cornelius Tacitus (56 – 117 AD)

Deciding how to deal with employees or contractors with negative background findings needs to be handled with sophistication, not by ham-handed methods. Adjudicating questionable findings should ideally be handled by committee, not by HR or the manager trying to hire the candidate, or to hold on to an existing employee.

With large organizations, VAers should ask if *anyone* has ever been rejected for hire or has been reassigned or placed under extra supervision when reliability questions later arise. If not, what is the point of the background checks, other than perhaps hoping that shady potential candidates will self-screen and won't apply for employment and/or that juries will be mollified when due diligence lawsuits are filed?

Organizations need to be particularly careful that employees do not have their careers ended by less than egregiously negative background checks. Ideally, the issues can be mitigated, or the employee can be transferred to a less sensitive position in the organization. The problem with terminating people with reliability questions is that this makes it less likely that other employees in the future will raise reliability concerns about coworkers. We certainly want to avoid the unintended consequences that often happen with, for example, government security clearances where employees are afraid to seek out marriage or other mental health counseling because they worry about losing their security clearance as a result. That isn't good for security (or for the organization or the employee).

With a background check, a history of minor crimes in one's youth should probably not be particularly damning. Nearly 1 in 3 adult Americans have an official criminal record, and the vast majority of Americans have committed unprosecuted crime in their lifetime.

It is important to realize that polygraphs ("lie detectors") have no role to play in a background check. Take a look at the science! Polygraphs are pseudo-scientific nonsense that belong in the same category as horoscopes, physiognomy, and psychic readings. They aren't even allowed in most courts. Many major U.S. spies caught in the past few decades passed polygraphs multiple times. Using polygraphs on candidates being considered for hire is, in my view, especially ignorant, foolish, racist, and sexist given the research showing polygraph exam bias. Nevertheless—amazingly—over half of law enforcement agencies still use pre-employment polygraph screening. A lot of innocent, quality candidates get permanently barred from law enforcement work from one arbitrary polygraph exam.

When people fill out background check information forms, or other employee forms, keep in mind that research shows people will be more honest if they sign a loyalty, ethics, or honesty pledge at the top of a form before they answer questions, rather than at the bottom, as is traditional.

Mitigation of Inadvertent Insider Threats

Vulnerability Assessors (VAers) should understand there are two kinds of insider threat: deliberate and inadvertent. The most prevalent and underestimated insider threat for most organizations is inadvertent—errors made by insiders (e.g., succumbing to phishing attacks) out of ignorance, incompetence, laziness, or carelessness.

Grey's / Schryver's Law: Any sufficiently advanced incompetence is indistinguishable from malice.

This is why VAers, when looking at inadvertent insider threats, need to pay attention to employee security awareness training, plus training on security use protocols. VAers need to keep in mind that adversaries may attempt to modify such training, as this can be a very effective way to introduce new vulnerabilities. The training curricula need to be protected from tampering! Few organizations do this.

While many security experts disparage security awareness training, I believe it can be a useful tool for countering inadvertent insider threats, but only if done well. Effective security awareness training is not about threatening, intimidating, patronizing, insulting, or boring employees. It should not, as is often the case, be taught by tedious, deadwood employees with no experience or common sense about security. Rather, security awareness training needs to motivate and educate employees about security, and ask for their help. It needs to show what is in it for them, and why security matters to the organization. The training needs to prepare employees and contractors to raise security questions and concerns, and make it clear that doing so is their duty.

Good security awareness training includes tips for securing the home and home computers/electronics. Advice needs to be given about how to avoid personal problems with ID theft, financial fraud, and travel hazards. Security awareness training must be engaging and fine-tuned to the audience. No one-size-fits all! Technical and highly-educated personnel need different guidance than low-level hourly workers.

Rather than be full of negative terms and warnings, security awareness training should emphasize the positive: how to get things done while still having good security. There should be specific examples. All of the following should be avoided: platitudes, organizational charts, references to federal CFRs, videos of talking-head camera-challenged executives, and self-serving fluff from HR, the security department, or the training department. Generally, less is more. It is important for the training to stick to the most important risks and how to mitigate them. There also needs to be training for all employees on how to deal with active shooters, and about how domestic violence may be brought into the workplace. Clear-cut information on how to contact the security help line must be provided.

Security awareness training ought to refer to stories about security breaches in other organizations and the consequences to people and the organization. The effectiveness and employees' opinion of the training should also be measured.

Insiders definitely need to be taught about social engineering. **Social Engineering** means to compromise security through psychological means. This includes adversaries using persuasion, seduction, coercion, blackmail, phishing, and other trickery. Insiders should also be warned that adversaries often conduct espionage using:
- impersonation
- clubs and social networking sites
- bogus headhunters and job interviews
- hanging out at nearby restaurants/bars
- phony trade journal interviews and industry "surveys"
- compromise of the public affairs, graphics, or copy departments because of their access to a lot of inside information
- recruitment of crafts people, custodians, telephone repairers, and secretaries
- targeting based on ethnicity, religion, veteran status, or foreign associations

The following is a checklist of key attributes for effective security awareness training, which can help mitigate insider risk and engender a healthy Security Culture:

1. Keep in mind that we train dogs. People we motivate, educate, and remind.

2. Be interesting, fun, engaging. No tedious computer training or boring, deadwood instructors! No one-size-fits all! Training for the Ph.D. research staff shouldn't be identical to that for the guys in the mail room.

3. Stick to the key points, don't bury people in minutiae. (But provide a truly helpful security help line to call or link to.)

4. Don't threaten or just talk about what <u>not</u> to do. Instead, talk about how to get things done productively AND securely.

5. Be sure to motivate all security rules (and have sunset reviews to see if rules are out of date). It's actually helpful to be honest about some rules and say, "Well, this rule is open for debate about its merits for our particular security, but we have to follow it to stay out of trouble." This is a vaccine against employee cynicism about security.

6. Don't emphasize compliance-based security (which is an oxymoron). Compliance-based security is not good security, it is control, which often gets confused with security. Be more like (good) *Safety* Awareness Training that emphasizes personal responsibility and alertness over just mindlessly following rules.

7. Make it clear: the security auditors, your security professionals, (and Vulnerability Assessors) are not the enemy. The bad guys are the enemy!

8. Give compelling examples of bad consequences for other organizations and their employees when security failed, including from insider attacks.

9. Discuss personal security at home and on travel; this sends the message that security is a good thing. Besides, with COVID-19, lots of work is now at home and will continue to be even post-COVID.

10. Have lively discussions about "What ifs?" (including about social engineering attacks) and free sharing of ideas. Don't just do "What ifs?" about compliance and following rules. Introducing some crazy "What if?" scenarios can be fun, and also gets people thinking more deeply about being prepared for the unexpected.

11. Avoid giving the impression there is always one right answer—consistency and groupthink are often confused with quality by bureaucrats. With security, local solutions are often the best solutions because the devil is always in the details.

12. Don't solely have information flowing downward. Collect useful upward flowing data. This is a chance to listen for new ideas, do sanity checks on security rules, seek employee pushback, and allow venting. The amount of intelligent pushback by employees is a good security metric and a measure of the health of a Security Culture —more is usually better within reason.

Mitigation of Deliberate Insider Threats

One issue that VAers need to closely examine when studying the security of an organization is the turnover rate for frontline security personnel (including "guards" and IT support). Turnover rates of 40% to 400% per year are not uncommon. A high turnover rate is a serious insider threat issue because it means there are large numbers of likely disgruntled security personnel who have left with detailed, sensitive security information about the organization and its vulnerabilities. A high-turnover rate suggests a problem with incompetent or bullying security supervisors and managers. It is also a serious economic and morale issue for the organization.

> *People don't leave jobs, they leave jerks.*
> -- old adage

Ideally, frontline security officers are giving realistic job descriptions at the time of hire that honestly explain the downsides of the job. Research shows this reduces the turnover rate. Psychological tests to determine if a person is suited for that kind of work may also be useful. New employees should be read into the organizational culture and values before cynical old-timers get to them. Other techniques for reducing disgruntlement for frontline security personnel are not so different from those for reducing general employee disgruntlement, discussed below.

Certainly treating everybody well—not just security personnel—is one of the most important countermeasures to insider threats. The reason is that disgruntlement, while not the only motivating factor, is a common driver for deliberate insider attacks. Moreover, disgruntlement is something that can actually be countered, unlike many other motivating factors. For example, how can you counter greed—another common motivating factor? If you pay employees more, they will just want more. Countermeasures for disgruntlement are not just effective but are also some of the least painful of all countermeasures available for mitigating deliberate insider threats. And they improve the overall organization, not just its security.

> *A mule will labor ten years willingly and patiently*
> *for you for the privilege of kicking you once.*
> -- William Faulkner (1897-1962)

The table below lists many of the motivating factors for insider attacks, along with some potential countermeasures.

Motivation for Deliberate Inside Attack	Possible Countermeasures
revenge	disgruntlement mitigation, track production deviance, watch for domestic violence being brought into the workplace
greed/financial need	periodic background checks, securing inventory, drug testing?, bribery anti-stings?
terrorism	periodic background checks, checking social media, staying alert
ideology, political activism, or radicalism	periodic background checks, checking social media, staying alert
coercion/blackmail	periodic background checks, planning

Motivation for Deliberate Inside Attack	Possible Countermeasures
social engineering/seduction	education
narcissism, self-aggrandization, ego, need to feel smart or special	enlist narcissists in VA, ego-stroke them
desire to prove that a warned about vulnerability or threat is real (Cassandra Effect)	ego stroke, enlist in VA, take security concerns seriously, welcome & listen to their criticisms
desire for excitement, would-be hero	make job more interesting? enlist in VA, ego stroke
mental illness?	periodic background checks, employee counseling and assistance programs, staying alert
inadvertent compromise of security	educate, motivate, reward good practices; don't punish if truly inadvertent

(Keep in mind, however, that there is little evidence that mental illness is a major motivator for insider attacks except for violent attacks. For example, one of the dozens of spies caught in the United States in the past 5 decades were mentally ill—despicable traitorous narcissists to be sure, but narcissism shouldn't really be considered a mental illness.)

So what specific techniques for mitigating disgruntlement should VAers look for or recommend to an organization? Basically, everybody should be treated well. This includes all insiders, but especially retirees, employees who have resigned, and even employees who have been fired. It is foolish and dangerous to give these people additional motivation to retaliate. In many organizations, HR and senior managers claim to treat employees "fairly" but this is often code for treating everybody consistently and equally badly.

In theory, HR can be a powerful tool for mitigating disgruntlement and reducing insider risk. In practice, however, HR often makes things worse by retaliating against disgruntled employees, scapegoating, condoning bad/bully bosses, ignoring sexual and racial harassment, and permitting a hostile work environment. Too often, HR is the secret police, torturer, judge, jury, and executioner.

VAers should evaluate HR performance from the standpoint of security and disgruntlement mitigation. VAers have a responsibility to warn about the security risks and vulnerabilities of having no constraints on HR tyranny, evil, arrogance, and charlatanism.

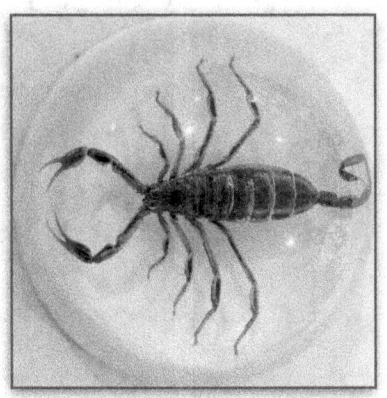

Traditionally, if HR Departments are evaluated at all by an organization, they are usually evaluated from a business, management, or compensation/benefits perspective —not from a security perspective. External VAers may be able to evaluate and challenge HR more safely than internal assessors.

Quite often, security practices are a tradeoff with employee productivity and morale. Good HR conduct, however, is a win-win.

> *The human-resources trade long ago proved itself, at best, a necessary evil—and at worst, a dark bureaucratic force that blindly enforces nonsensical rules, resists creativity, and impedes constructive change.*
> -- Keith H. Hammonds

VAers should also examine whether HR and managers/supervisors in general recognize that whatever an employee or contractor says is upsetting him/her probably isn't the real issue. And is the 80% rule routinely used? The 80% rule of thumb states that if someone with even minimal authority will simply **listen, empathize, and validate** when there is an upset employee and let him/her vent—even if they don't happen to agree with the employee and don't fix the problem—the employee will feel better about himself, the organization, and the problem 80% of the time. This can be a cheap and effective anti-disgruntlement technique. (Though, of course, a sincere attempt to fix the problem bugging the employee can go even further towards reducing disgruntlement!)

One thing that security professionals can potentially do is to intervene formally or informally when they see HR, managers, or supervisors bully or behave in other ways that are detrimental to security. Perhaps a security professional could do the missing listening, empathizing, and validating, or the necessary ego stroking of narcissists or Cassandras. Similarly, if it becomes clear that an employee is not having his or her unique psychological issues addressed, proactive security professionals may need to at least try to flag or rectify the situation.

The security professional's conversation with the disgruntled employee needs to be handled with a certain finesse. If the employee thinks you are there to check up on them (which partially, you are), this may not be helpful. Instead, the security professional can say something along the lines of the following: "Look, I'm not concerned about you. You're an ethical professional well respected around here, except perhaps by the person(s) hassling you. But sometimes in our organization, employees don't get treated very well and employees with less class than you can become a security concern. Thus, I like to keep a tab on employee mistreatment anywhere in the organization, applied to anybody. Why don't you tell me about your situation?"

[Note that telling the employee he/she is well respected may require some embellishment, but almost everybody is liked by somebody, even if it is just by the food truck vendor in the parking lot. Note also that these words, which aren't put in print, can put the security professional and the organization at some risk should there be litigation, but the counter-argument is that every security professional is entitled to her own opinion.]

Organizations can even establish formal mechanisms (including the use of employee advocates) to help security professionals raise red flags about existing or potential disgruntlement cases. Of course, the penalty flag needs to be thrown against misbehaving HR, managers, and supervisors, not against the employee in question.

Security professionals throughout the organization (including IT support personnel) need to informally chat up employees on a regular basis to gather information on local conditions and problems. This is also useful for establishing friendly working relations. Security professionals should always present themselves as being there to help work get done securely. They should not play the role of thugs, enforcers, or the secret police. Accordingly, VAers might want to examine how regular employees feel about security personnel in the organization.

For all employees, disgruntlement is more about unmet expectations than objective fact. Employees who are badly treated but expect to be, are not necessarily a disgruntlement risk. Organizations need to be especially careful about badly managing expectations of technical and other highly-skilled or educated personnel. These kind of employees often expect to be consulted on important issues and decisions facing the enterprise. The can become quite angry if this is not the case.

HR should especially avoid the traditional, sadistic "perp walk" where fired employees are paraded past their former co-workers under escort by security officers. Terminated employees need to be treated with privacy and respect, regardless of what they have done. It is stupid to give them more reasons to retaliate.

All organizations should have effective grievance complaint processes in place that are fair, and widely viewed as such by employees. Many grievance programs are really just a process for disgruntled employees to self-identify for purposes of retaliation. Having an independent employee/contractor advocate should also be considered.

The most relevant metric for a grievance complaint process is how often it gets used. If the process is not much used, that is not a sign of a healthy organization (as HR and senior managers like to claim). Rather, it is evidence that employees have figured out that the grievance process is phony, ineffective, and/or dangerous.

VAers ought to check if the organization has effective and safe employee assistance and counseling programs. These can help employees with personal problems, financial and medical crises, mental health matters, alcoholism and drug addiction, etc. Such programs can help to reduce the insider threat. Ideally, these programs are outsourced and independent, rather than being run by HR thugs.

VAers should also be on the lookout for phony or non-existent anonymous whistle blower programs and anonymous tip hot lines. VAers may also want to look at employee morale. This affects the insider risk via disgruntlement.

Organizations should be encouraged to publicly prosecute insider offenders who have committed serious attacks, and make their alleged misdeeds known to coworkers. Many organizations shy away from this for "privacy" reasons, to avoid negative publicity about the organization's possibly negligent security, and out of fear of the legal discovery process. This, however, is cowardice, not prudence. If the worst that an insider attacker faces is the quiet loss of a job, there is little disincentive not to attack. Some organizations are even afraid to give negative job recommendations for their fired employees who have committed significant crimes while attacking!

VAers need to encourage organizations to search in the outside world to determine if any of their intellectual property or trade secrets have escaped into the wild. In one sense, the horse has already left the barn, but finding out you have been burned at least allows you to prosecute, change your business plans, and examine what went wrong with your security.

VAers should examine whether the organization pays special attention to employees, contractors, or vendors who think (rightly or wrongly) they may soon be gone or have their funding or responsibilities cut, or who don't receive expected tenure, promotions, or honors. Similarly, organizations need to closely watch for the common precursors to insider attacks, which are sudden changes in:

- hygiene
- attitude
- performance
- rule compliance
- interest in weapons
- use of drugs or alcohol
- being late for work or a no-show
- aggression, hostility, racism
- not getting along with coworkers or the boss
- behaviors that seem out of character
- behaviors that make coworkers or the boss uncomfortable

The key concept here is <u>sudden changes</u>. Many employees will consistently have at least some of these negative characteristics or character flaws throughout their career but won't ever attack. And only a small minority of employees with the above sudden changes will actually undertake malicious activities.

Organizations often overlook the insider threat from relatively low-level employees who work security issues, or have access to sensitive information. This includes personnel who create documents and security badges, schedule guard shifts, handle work orders, grant access privileges, administer drug testing and records, book meeting rooms and virtual teleconferences, and make or have access to travel schedules.

Other issues VAers should consider is whether the organization uses role-based access control. Are access privileges <u>instantly</u> updated when an employee or contractor is promoted, reassigned, or terminated? Are access privileges frequently reviewed to see if they are out of date? VAers should encourage the organization to think about which employees/contractors/positions are most likely to be targeted by adversaries for compromise, and those who have the most risky insider access.

VAers should warn organization about not being prepared for active shooters and domestic violence coming into the workplace.

VAers should encourage bright lighting in sensitive areas, having visually open but acoustically closed interior architecture when sensitive work is being done, and keeping photocopiers and printers in visually open, uncluttered areas. Remarkably, research shows that if a poster with angry eyes is placed in work areas, employees will behave more honestly. They feel as if they are being watched, though it is a totally subconscious phenomenon. This should only be used in sensitive or classified work areas, or for increasing contributions to the coffee fund.

Other issues that VAers need to study are whether thorough exit interviews are being done when employees leave, and if interviews are done with candidates who turn down job offers. Much can be learned about insider risks and other issues by doing this.

VAers should check for poor drug testing security. Most urine testing programs (government, companies, sports) have poor security protocols; it is actually quite easy to tamper with urine test kits, for example. Drug test samples or results can be tampered with by insiders or outsiders (including when a third-party drug testing service is used). This can be for the purpose of discrediting key personnel or protecting illegal drug users. Historically, the emphasis has been on false negatives, but false positives are equally troubling for security. The traditionally poor security for drug testing in general has serious implications for safety, the courts, public welfare, national security, fairness, careers, livelihood, reputations, and sports.

In thinking about insider threat, it is very important not to focus solely on the idea that the insider must be a full, active participant in the attack or theft. Sometimes an insider may simply feed outsiders some key information that makes an attack more feasible, or can be bribed or threatened to look the other way during an attack. It is widely believed, for example, that 80% of all truck cargo thefts entail some involvement by the driver. He may be paid a bribe simply not to put up a struggle during a truck hijacking and/or to mislead the police. Security guards for warehouse/loading dock areas are sometimes paid to be elsewhere or on a break during a heist.

Though rarely done—because most organizations lack the cajones—I am a big fan of **bribery anti-stings**. In a regular bribery sting operation, law enforcement or security officials target suspected corrupt individuals to see if they can be bribed. In a bribery anti-sting, you target suspected honest insiders, or else randomly select insiders. After some initial cozying-up, they are offered a bribe to conduct, assist, or ignore malicious activity. If the person rejects the bribe and reports it (which is what we hope for), they get to keep the money. They are then widely praised and publicized as a hero.

A bribery anti-sting only needs to be done every few years in order to undercut adversaries' ability to execute bribes. Insiders will be hesitant to accept a bribe because they will suspect it might be a test, and they don't want to blow their chance to keep the money. This is not so much the case with regularly bribery stings because even corrupt employees don't necessarily picture themselves as corrupt or a target.

There are caveats to this approach. The target should be allowed <u>at least</u> 2 days to report or reject the bribe. The organization must provide clear, frequently publicized, and easy to find guidelines about the need to report a bribery attempt, and exactly who to report it to. After a successful anti-sting, it should be made widely known within the organization that the person was chosen for the bribery because he/she was assumed honest, or because his/her name was drawn out of a hat. There are legal entrapment issues here, but the goal is not to fire or arrest people (as in a sting operation), but rather to undercut the effectiveness of future bribery attempts.

Another issue worth considering is the 2-person rule. This is commonly used in critical security programs like nuclear security, or for financial transactions. The idea is that we might be able to lower insider risk if an attack requires 2 people to go rogue instead of 1. Intuitively, the idea of a 2-person rule would seem to make sense. There is, however, limited supporting research. (This is true even for nuclear security where the 2-person rule was originally developed for safety, not security reasons.) Some of the research that does exist suggests that people may actually be MORE likely to cheat when the benefits can be split with another person due to less guilt.

The two people in a 2-person team should be changed fairly often. There needs to be clear-cut guidance on when to report a fellow team member, how, and to whom. Occasionally, one team member should be tested by having the other act suspiciously or crazily to test the response.

The organization should take a close look at an employee who never takes time off. He or she may be hesitant to miss work out of fear that their embezzlement or other misdeeds might be detected.

Work schedules and work orders for employees and security guard round assignments need to be carefully protected from tampering.

VAers should also be aware of research that shows that income affects unethical behavior. Wealthy individuals are more likely to behave unethically than low-income people. When a wealthy person does something unethical, it is usually to help only himself. When poor people do something unethical, it is often to help out their family or other poor people. This suggest a strategy for trying to prevent insider attacks: With high-salary employees, warn about the harm to themselves if caught. Give examples from other organizations of what happened to high-level employees who were found out. With lower income employees, emphasize the harm to their coworkers and family, and to the organization if they engage in bad behavior. Give examples of where this has happened elsewhere.

Security engineers and security managers sometimes dismiss the above psychological or sociological measures for mitigating insider threat as "merely" soft approaches. The word "soft" is meant to be dismissive, as in "soft on crime" or "soft on Russia". The fact is, however, that insider threat is a largely psychological and sociological matter and requires such approaches. Technology certainly has a role to play in helping with insider threat mitigation but is is only a tool, not a solution.

Some final insider threat issues that VAers should take a look at, or at least get their sponsor or client to consider:

- Arson is a surprisingly common and destructive kind of insider attack by disgruntled insiders, so don't leave flammable chemicals laying around unsecured. Have adequate smoke and fire detectors in the facility that can't be easily disabled.

- Malicious insiders frequently try to frame coworkers. Any investigation of a security incident should explore whether there are coworkers who held strong grudges against the suspected culprit.

- Watch out for family members or spouses who work for the same organization. They may collaborating in mischief, or covering up for each other.

- Except for small organizations, the same person (or their spouse or relative) should never work in more than one of the following departments: Accounts Payable, Accounts Receivable, Procurement, Shipping, Receiving, or the Mail Room. Otherwise, there are just too many opportunities for mischief.

- The amount of industrial espionage that takes place in the United States is grossly underestimated by most companies.

- Watch out for supervisors and manages who have power but relatively low status or reputation. They are at especially high risk for being bullies and creating disgruntlement.

- Secure or monitor the trash! The trash is often used by insider attackers to sneak things in or out of facilities. And outsiders may "dumpster dive" for information.

- Ban private vehicles from loading dock areas unless monitored or supervised.

- Mail rooms and utility closets need to be secured.

- Many organizations use deceit and heavy-handed intimidation when interviewing employees after a serious security incident, such as a theft. The interrogators may falsely tell a suspect that a co-worker has fingered them, or that there is video showing the suspect engaged in the attack. This is done in hopes of eliciting a confession. Such despicable, un-American, and ethically bankrupt practices are especially common after retail theft, and often lead to false confessions. This kind of thuggery can create enormous damage to the organization's Security Culture, and to employe trust and morale. The hypocrisy of security professionals (or police officers) looking for and demanding the truth while lying to get it is truly cringe-worthy.

Factoid: Out of 30 million known species of bacteria, only about 70 cause disease.

Chapter 11 Discussion and Thought Questions

1. What other motivations for insider attacks can you think of that are not in the table?

2. Why do you think the countermeasures listed in the table would work? How would you actually implement each of them?

3. What other countermeasures might help reduce the risk of insider attacks?

4. Do some research on the Internet or in the library, and find research papers and discussions of the following issues: (a) problems with polygraphs and other conventional methods for "lie detection"; (b) new technology under development that might be more effective for "lie detector" (but watch out for hype and snake oil!); (c) the use of angry eyes on posters to make people more honest; (d) the difference between wealthy and poor people in terms of ethical behavior; (e) signing an honesty oath at the top of a document is more effective than signing it at the bottom; (f) examples of and motivations for past insider attacks and the consequences of the

attacks; and/or (g) known examples of national security espionage and industrial espionage, and what can be learned from them.

5. If a security manager finds that HR, or non-security managers and supervisors in the organization are mistreating employees in a way that puts security at risk, what can she do about it? What are the career risks to doing so?

6. What are the pros and cons of doing a bribery anti-sting? How about a regular bribery sting operation?

7. Why is it a good idea to prosecute major insider attackers in court and transparently alert his/her coworkers to what is going on, yet treat the attacker well during and after firing them, including no "perp walk"?

8. If someone is a suspect in an insider attack, how should investigators go about trying to figure out if they might have been framed?

9. Why are dishonest and intimidating interviewing techniques after a security incident extremely risky for the health of the organization's Security Culture and employee morale? Are they even ethical? (In many Western democracies, but not so much it the USA, it is illegal for police to lie to suspects or witnesses.)

10. Why is it a bad idea to have the same person (or his/her spouse or relative) work in more than one of these departments: Accounts Payable, Accounts Receivable, Procurement, Shipping, Receiving, or the Mail Room? What kind of attacks are more likely if this advice is not followed?

11. What are the pros and cons of proprietary guards (employees) versus contract guards (outsourced)? Which is typically less expensive? Which is better in terms of turnover and insider threat risk?

12. Why should private vehicles be banned from the area of loading docks, unless monitored or supervised?

13. How would you use unsecured or unmonitored trash to attack the organization, either as an insider or as an outsider? How could an adversary exploit an unsecured mail room?

Chapter 12. Security Reasoning Errors

Whenever there is a simple error that most laymen fall for, there is always a slightly more sophisticated version of the same problem that experts fall for.

-- Amos Tversky (1937-1996)

There are a number of classic fallacies in reasoning that can harm security. They can negatively impact how we think about, and how we discuss security. Avoiding these logical errors can help with clarity of thought as well as increase our objectivity.

Some of these fallacies include:

Argument from Consequences Fallacy: This is where bad consequences of a certain course of action are assumed. The consequences may be likely or not, but in any case, they do not speak directly to the merits of the proposed action. Often used in politics. Common examples in security: (1) It would be very bad if we had security vulnerabilities so therefore we do not. (2) Critics of election security reform use this kind of false argument, claiming that any discussion of election security vulnerabilities undermines faith in democracy. (3) Control often gets confused with Security.

Appeal to Fear Fallacy: This is warning of a bad consequence for which there is insufficient evidence. Common example in security: Security sales pitches.

p	q	$p \rightarrow q$ (conditional)	$q \rightarrow p$ (converse)	$\sim p \rightarrow \sim q$ (inverse)	$\sim q \rightarrow \sim p$ (contrapositive)
T	T	T	T	T	T
T	F	F	T	T	F
F	T	T	F	F	T
F	F	T	T	T	T

Slippery Slope Fallacy: Discrediting an idea by arguing that its acceptance will lead to a series of events that are undesirable. This fallacy typically assumes that the envisioned events are inevitable, even though no evidence is offered. It is related to the Appeal to Fear Fallacy. Common example in security: Ironically, this fallacy is often used by people on both sides of the argument about the alleged need for greater national security versus the potential negative impact on privacy, civil liberties, and adherence to the Bill of Rights.

Straw Man Fallacy: This involves misrepresenting an idea as something more ludicrous than the actual idea. Often used in politics. Common example in security: Frequently used to argue against a potential new countermeasure or change in security.

Appeal to Irrelevant Authority Fallacy: The views of those who are not credible experts on the subject are cited as strong evidence. Common examples in security: (1) The sales guy says this security product is really good. (2) This security product or strategy is used a lot by _____ so therefore we need to use it, too. (3) This security product is high-tech so it must be good. (4) The engineers can't figure out how to defeat this security device so it must be good. (In fact, however, engineers typically have the wrong mindset and experience to perform effective Vulnerability Assessments.)

Equivocation Fallacy: This involves changing the meaning of a word. The new meaning is then used to reason or argue a wrong conclusion. This type of argument is used by lawyers all the time. Common examples in security: (1) Vulnerabilities often get confused with threats or assets needing protection, and with facility features. (2) Vulnerability Assessments are often confused with Threat Assessments, security surveys, compliance auditing, performance testing, pen(etration) testing, and "Red Teaming". (3) Measurements of inventory are often confused with security measures, even when they make no significant effort to counter spoofing. (4) Calling a security product "high security" when that is the intended application for the product or a complex value judgement, not an attribute of the product.

False Dilemma (Black & White or False Dichotomy) Fallacy: Only 2 possibilities are presented with no others allowed, including shades of gray. Common examples in security: (1) Security is often thought of as binary—we are secure or we are not. In reality, security is a continuum. The idea of "gap analysis" unfortunately plays to this binary mindset. (2) We hired a convicted criminal, gave him a crowbar, and he couldn't defeat the security device. Therefore, the device is undefeatable.

Not a Cause for a Cause Fallacy: Assuming a cause for an event when there is no evidence for such a thing. There are actually 2 kinds: correlation getting confused with causation, and *post hoc, ergo propter hoc,* which is an event preceding another event that is incorrectly thought to be the cause of that second event. Common examples in security: (1) There were no serious security incidents recently so that must mean our security is great. (2) Scapegoating after security incidents.

Hasty Generalization Fallacy: Conclusions are drawn from too small or specialized a sample. Common examples in security: (1) We can't immediately identify any obvious vulnerabilities. Therefore there are none and our security is excellent. (2) We did a Red Team exercise "testing" one specific attack so we therefore fully understand our security vulnerabilities and no attacks need be of concern.

Appeal to Ignorance Fallacy: A proposition is claimed to be true because there is no evidence it is false. Absence of evidence is incorrectly taken to be evidence of absence. A special version of this fallacy is Argument From Personal Incredulity—I can't see how this proposition can be true so this means it is false. Common examples in security: (1) I've seen no evidence that this security device or program can be defeated; therefore it cannot be. (2) I (a non-expert) can't envision how to defeat this security (especially since I don't want to) so therefore nobody can.

Circular Reasoning Fallacy: A kind of begging the question where we assume the conclusion is one of the premises. Often the conclusion is reworded to disguise it. "You are wrong because you are not making any sense" is an example. Common example in security: We've had no tampering because no tampered seals were discovered. (The flaw in the argument, however, is that—by definition—spoofed seals are not detected.)

No True Scotsman Fallacy: After a general claim about a group of things, a counter example is found. Then, that thing is declared not part of the group or not a "true" member. This fallacy is related to the Circular Reasoning Fallacy. (The name of the fallacy comes from the idea that no "true" Scotsman would ever say or do a certain thing, so that if a given gentleman does, he cannot therefore be a true Scotsman even if he is a Scotsman.) Common example in security: That attack was demonstrated on Thursday but today is Tuesday. Therefore, the attack isn't viable today.

Genetic (Questioning Motives) Fallacy: An idea or proposition is devalued or defended solely based on its source or origins. Common examples in security: (1) The motives and loyalty of vulnerability assessors or stakeholders who ask questions about security are questioned as a way of rejecting their concerns. (2) The higher ups made this security rule so it must be a good idea.

Guilt by Association Fallacy: Discrediting an idea solely because it is held by a demonized group. This is a kind of *non sequitur*. It falsely assumes that accepting the idea would make one automatically part of the evil group. Common example in security: They use these tactics in Russia, China, or Iran, so therefore we should not.

Affirming the Consequent (Converse) Fallacy: We know that "if A, then C" is true. We know that C is true. Therefore, A is true. This is false reasoning. Common examples in security: (1) If we treat our employees well, they will be less likely to engage in insider attacks. We haven't detected any insider attacks. Therefore, we are treating our employees well. (2) If we have no adversaries, we won't be attacked. We haven't been attacked recently. Therefore, we have no adversaries.

Appeal to Hypocrisy (Tu Quoque = "You Too") Fallacy: Claiming that an advocate for a given idea or proposition has shown past inconsistency in thought, argument, or deed. This diverts attention from the truth or falsehood of the idea or proposition in question. Often used in politics. Common example in security: This security manager was once a strong proponent of using contract guards but now uses proprietary guards, so her views on security awareness training are highly suspect.

Appeal to the Bandwagon (Appeal to the People) Fallacy: If a lot of people believe in something, it must be true. Common examples in security: (1) Nobody else seems to be worried about these kinds of attacks, so we shouldn't be either. (2) The government and the police uses polygraphs a lot so they must be valid.

Ad Hominem ("To the Man") Argument Fallacy: Attack the proponent of an idea (including his qualifications and assumed motivation), rather than the idea itself. Common example in security: This argument is often used to discredit vulnerability assessors, security critics, and those proposing unconventional security strategies.

Composition Fallacy: Because part of a whole has an attribute, the whole must, too. Common examples in security: (1) We encrypt or digitally authenticate the data so that rules out theft, tampering, or sabotage. (2) Because we use good locks, we must have good security overall. (3) The security device uses a lock, a seal, a mechanical tamper switch, or "tamper proof" screws, therefore it cannot be tampered with.

Division Fallacy: One part of a whole must have a certain attribute because the whole does. Common examples in security: (1) Our security has held up well. Therefore, all parts are fully optimized. (2) We use layered security ("defense in depth"). Therefore, the effectiveness of any given layer isn't of concern.

Cognitive Dissonance Fallacy: Our reasoning is negatively impacted by the mental tension generated by ideas or facts we do not wish to be true or to contemplate. Poorly handled cognitive dissonance is probably a key cause of bad security across a wide range of security applications. This can lead to Security Theater; wishful thinking; denial and wishful ignorance (deliberately avoiding facing the facts); stagnation/paralysis (not addressing problems); self justification (self-serving rationalization and excuse making); confirmation bias and motivated reasoning (incorrectly interpreting data in ways that make us feel good); and invoking any number of the above fallacies. Common examples in security: (1) We have no serious vulnerabilities. (2) Our employees are too loyal to attack. (3) HR says we have an effective employee complaint/grievance process.

Fallacy of Precision: The belief that assigning a numeric value to something means we have a full understanding of it, or that semi-arbitrarily assigned numbers impart rigor. Common examples in security: (1) Believing uncritically in risk probabilities that are often only semi-educated guesses, old news about the past, or just wishful thinking. (2) Hiring one candidate over another because he/she has a slightly higher GPA three digits right of the decimal even though the candidates attended different schools, studied different subjects, took courses with varying degrees of difficulty, and had completely different teachers/professors.

The more you can recognize and avoid these reasoning and argument errors, the better your security is likely to be!

> *Whenever, therefore, people are deceived and form opinions wide of the truth, it is clear that the error has slid into their minds through the medium of certain resemblances to that truth.*
>
> -- Socrates (469 – 399 BC)

Note: a version of this Chapter first appeared in my paper in *Journal of Physical Security* **10**(1), 86-90 (2017).

<u>Chapter 12 Discussion and Thought Questions</u>

1. What examples of these various logical reasoning errors have you seen (a) in your organization, (b) in your personal life and among your friends and relatives, (c) in security, (d) in politics, and (e) in yourself?

Chapter 13. Attacks on Security Hardware

Every wall is a door.
-- Ralph Waldo Emerson (1803-1882)

This chapter briefly summarizes some of the more important and effective attacks that Vulnerability Assessors need to consider. There are almost an unlimited number of possible attacks on security hardware. In the case of tags and seals, for example, I have identified 105 different generic attack categories for tamper-indicating seals and 91 for tags. See *Journal of Nuclear Materials Management* **229**, 23-30 (2000). I suspect, however, that I missed a number of attack categories.

Cyber Attack: There are, of course, lots of cyber hacking kinds of attacks possible on security devices and their microprocessors or microcontrollers. Many of these do not typically require a sophisticated understanding of most of the technical details of how the device or system operates.

Manipulation Attack: These are attacks analogous to picking a lock. The security device is defeated or spoofed using the existing openings in the case, perhaps with the aid of custom-made tools. Alternately, the security device may be manipulated with electromagnetic waves or other energy. Manipulation Attacks work well against a surprising number of security devices, including high-tech ones.

Invasive Manipulation Attack: One or more small openings are made in the case. These are used to complete a Manipulation Attack and then repaired, either cosmetically or thoroughly. Repairs such as done by auto body repair technicians and art/antique restorers can be very effective.

Manufacturer Installed Backdoor: A particularly difficult kind of attack to detect is when the adversary manufactures the security product. He puts in a "backdoor" into the product at the design or manufacturing stage. A backdoor is some kind of software, firmware, electronics, or mechanical feature installed by the adversary that allows him to (a) grab control of the device or system when desired, or (2) shut it down at appropriate times, or (3) more easily attack the hardware once it is put in place by the end-user. Backdoors can be put in at chip level, in the firmware or software, at the printed circuit board level, or even built into the case of the device.

Tampering: For this attack, the adversary modifies a security product that he did not manufacture. The attack can be for a number of purposes such as installing a backdoor, inserting some other kind of hardware or software defect, disabling the device, or stealing algorithm or encryption key information. This attack can be executed at the factory, vendor, while the product is in transit, at the loading dock, while in storage, before the product is installed by the end-user, or after it is installed. I know from first-hand experience that a skilled attacker with a considerable practice and specially designed tools can complete the tampering within 15 seconds for many security devices.

Man-in-the-Middle (MiM) Attack: This is a kind of tampering attack that (typically) requires very brief physical access to a security device or system just once (before or after the security product is installed by the end-user). MiM attacks are very effective against voting machines, tag and seal readers, motion detectors, biometrics, prox card readers, and other kinds of access control or monitoring devices. The adversary rarely needs to understand in detail how most of the security device or system works.

The idea with MiM attacks is that some alien electronics (e.g, a logic gate, microprocessor, or microcontroller) is inserted in the middle of one of the communications channels inside the security device or system. The MiM electronics can be spliced into the wires that transmit signals from a sensor to the microcontroller. Alternately, the alien MiM electronics might be inserted between the microprocessor and data storage, an encryption box, PIN entry keypad, etc. When desired, the adversary's alien MiM electronics will tamper with or block the signals. MiM also works well as a software attack, and for unencrypted wireless signals and even some encrypted wireless signals.

A particularly easy MiM attack (even for resourceful high school kids) is to control the ASCII input to a video screen or LCD display that the good guys view. Most of the time, the MiM electronics leave the display information alone. When needed, however, the electronics block the true display information and instead cause false information to be displayed, such as "everything is fine" status when everything is not fine. With this kind of MiM display attack, the adversary has to understand virtually nothing about how the rest of the device or system operates!

MiM attacks are often trivially easy against security devices that are supposed to issue some kind of alarm or "All OK" signal. The MiM electronics are designed by the adversary (potentially smart middle school kids) to block the alarm, but only when the adversary wishes it. The blocking may be done at predetermined times (e.g., 2AM every night when the facility is closed), or when the adversary sends an external wireless signal to his MiM electronics, or when the MiM microprocessor detects certain conditions.

A good countermeasure against MiM alarm attacks against motion detectors and burglar alarms is a Town Crier approach, where an encrypted bit or byte is sent continuously every few seconds or minutes to indicate everything is fine; the failure of some sequential number of these bits or bytes to show up is the alarm. An analogous Anti-Evidence approach works very well for electronic tags and tamper-indicating seals; rather than look for evidence of intrusion or counterfeiting, we check for the <u>absence</u> of the evidence indicating everything is fine.

With MiM attacks, it is of limited security value for good guys to check if the device or system seems to be operating properly—as is sometimes done with voting machines or access control devices. With a MiM attack, the security device or system *will* be operating normally most of the time, including during tests.

Tampering with the Use Protocol: This is a kind of tampering attack where the adversary modifies the security product's user manual, or the training on its use protocol done by the end-user. The intent is to introduce security vulnerabilities that can be exploited.

"Counterfeiting" a Security Device: Usually merely mimicking the superficial appearance and a few characteristics of the authentic device is adequate. The original device can be swapped out for a fake or tampered version. Alternately, just some of the components may be counterfeit. Most end-users have no way to detect if the security device they are using is the one they originally bought, and those that do have a way to check this rarely do.

Factoid: The great film comedian, Charlie Chaplin, once entered a Charlie Chaplin look-a-like contest for a laugh. To his surprise, he did not win.

Signal or Signature Counterfeiting: Such as making a copy of a fingerprint or a hologram tag. Another example is remotely sending a spoofing UV or IR signal to the reader of a fluorescent product anti-counterfeiting tag from less than 50 meters away.

Lifting: The security product is moved from one place to another or one container to another without any evidence being noticed that this has happened. Lifting attacks often work well for tags and seals. Adhesive label anti-counterfeiting tags and tamper-indicating seals are especially vulnerable.

Denial of Service Attack: With this attack, the device is damaged or normal operation is prevented using, for example, electromagnetic jamming, emf pulses, excessive data input, disconnection of the power, etc.

Sleepy Time Attack: With this attack, the microcontroller or a sensor is put to sleep temporarily by cutting off its power. Freezing the microprocessor or sensor, or freezing the battery is often effective, too. There are some easy countermeasures, but they are rarely implemented, or are implemented in an ineffective manner when they are used.

Time Slip Attack: This can be a very effective attack. The adversary tampers with the security device's idea of of what time it is, perhaps by tampering with its clock or spoofing the GPS time signal (which my team demonstrated in the early 1990s).

Other kinds of attacks or reverse-engineering techniques for security hardware that Vulnerability Assessors (and security engineers) need to consider include the following:

- false alarming until the end-user loses faith in the security device or system
- power analysis
- fault analysis
- buffer overflow
- divide by zero errors or saturation errors, including on a computed correlation coefficient
- exploiting state of health (SOH) diagnostics and reporting
- JTAG or other diagnostics not turned off
- thermal attacks
- solvent attacks
- side channel attacks
- breaking the cipher or data authentication hash
- wait and pounce attacks: waiting for anomalous conditions or distractions
- poke the system: study how security reacts when you do unexpected things

---

The bridge of the Starship Enterprise is always exploding with high voltage or plasma conduit discharges when under attack. What in the world were the designers thinking by running high voltage or plasma through or near the control consoles? What's wrong with 5-volt TTL logic or even photonics?

Chapter 13 Discussion and Thought Questions

1. What general countermeasures can you think of for each of the attacks discussed in this chapter?

2. How can time slip attacks be used to defeat security?

3. How can we determine if a backdoor has been built into an integrated circuit chip by a foreign manufacturer?

4. Why is merely testing to see if a security device or system seems to be working no guarantee that it hasn't been hijacked or tampered with?

5. How can you find alien MiM electronics inside a security device, given that very small, surface mount electronics can be easily added to a printed circuit board?

6. How can we determine when the outside of a security device or system has been cosmetically repaired after an attack?

Chapter 14. Other Security Tips

If you are happy with your security, so are the bad guys.
-- old adage

This Chapter offers assorted suggestions for better security that should be considered by both security managers and Vulnerability Assessors.

➢ Beware of unwarranted faith in layered security ("defense in depth"). Multiple layers of flawed security don't usually magically add up to good security. Layered security often results in over-confidence, laziness, sloppy thinking, complexity, and an unwillingness to make security improvements. It is often an excuse to avoid thinking critically about security. Security managers whose main security strategy is to have layered security are often blind to the ways in which different layers get in each others way, or don't truly back each other up, or share common failure modes. There is usually fuzzy thinking about what each layer is supposed to do, and which layers are targeted at what adversaries—they can't all work against all possible bad guys. With layered security, security guards don't get too excited about problems, anomalous events, or unauthorized personnel in any one layer because, "Hey, we have other layers". In addition, layered security tends to ignore the insider threat, and over emphasize brute force attacks. All of this is not to say that layered security isn't sometimes needed, just that it has issues.

➢ Most existing product anti-counterfeiting tags, tamper-evident packaging, and tamper-indicating seals are poorly designed, and their use protocols are even worse Security Theater. The terminology with seals is particularly appalling and misleading. Most (all?) tags and seals can be readily spoofed, counterfeited, or mimicked using low-tech methods, often by amateurs. Contact the author or see http://rbsekurity.com for information on how to choose tags and seals, and use them more better, and about the MUCH better designs that are possible.

Other Security Tips

➢ Don't confuse inventory with security. They are two very different functions. Confusing them leads to very bad security. Inventory systems are for counting and locating assets but do not have the security to detect or counter malicious spoofing. That is the job of security. Confusing inventory with security is the reason it has been historically easy to spoof GPS, RFIDs, contact memory buttons, prox cards, and nuclear material control and accountability equipment. Be especially wary of mission creep. Inventory systems are often initially recognized as having little security, but then very quickly come to be viewed as a security system to detect theft.

➢ Don't confuse high-tech with "high-security". In my experience, advanced technology is usually easy to defeat with low-tech attacks. Why is high-tech often so easy to defeat? The developers and users often lack street smarts about security and a proper security mindset and culture. They are focused on the wrong issues. There are many more legs to attack. Users don't understand the technology. The hardware or computer system still must be physically coupled to the real world. The security still depends on the loyalty and security competence of the user's personnel, as well as that of the developers, vendors, and manufacturers. The increased standoff distance decreases the user's attention to detail. The are problems with the "Titanic Effect", i.e., arrogance about high-tech.

➢ "High Security" is a context- and application-dependent value judgment, not a product attribute!

➢ VAers and security managers cannot be oblivious to security fatigue, where employees have simply become too overwhelmed by security training, tasks, and red tape.

129

➤ Beware of an over-emphasis on fences. Even "high-security" ones usually provide only 4.5 to 15 seconds of access delay.

➤ Put door hinges on the inside!

➤ So-called "security screws" are to discourage teenagers from disassembling restroom hardware. They provide no significant security.

➤ Mechanical tamper switches and light sensors offer no meaningful security for detecting intrusion into security devices or systems.

➤ Use of pressure-sensitive adhesive label seals by cyber personnel are almost always Security Theater.

➤ Just because you have a biometric or other access control device outside a door does not mean it has to be attacked or spoofed to gain entry. There are other ways into the room. (The bad guys get to define the security problem, not the good guys).

➤ Security devices should not contain a lot of empty space. This makes it easier for adversaries to hide alien electronics. Security devices also should not have a lot of unnecessary openings.

➤ Critical security devices should be opened periodically and examined for tampering and alien electronics. This requires having a (secured) photograph of what the insides of the device is supposed to look like.

➤ A secure chain of custody is essential for all security devices. Typically, a skilled and practiced adversary can gain control over a security device in about 15 seconds. This can be done during design, at the factory, at the vendor, in transit, on the loading dock, before installation at the end-user, or after installation. Testing to see if a security device operates normally is approximately worthless at spotting tampering.

➢ Most (all?) biometric access control devices have little security and can be readily spoofed or hijacked. Counterfeiting biometric signatures is also fairly straightforward but usually takes more work than attacking the device. "Liveness" detectors on biometrics are usually fairly easy to spoof.

➢ While only a partial countermeasure, biometric and access control devices should be periodically tested at random times with random people to be sure the devices don't let everybody in, authorized or not. Some attacks make the device accept anybody.

➢ Be aware that the reliability of facial recognition is over-hyped, facial biometrics can be spoofed (even 3D), and currently, females and minorities are not as well recognized as white males.

➢ Most security devices, including biometrics and other access control technology, are susceptible to these kinds of attacks:
- clone the signature of an authorized person
- do a man-in-the-middle (MM) attack
- access the password or key
- copy or tamper with the database
- "counterfeit" the device
- replace the microprocessor
- tamper with the software
- install a backdoor

➢ A key does not unlock a lock. It starts a sequence of actions that opens the lock.

➢ Don't become so focused on prevention (which is difficult at best) that you ignore effective planning for recovery after attacks.

➤ We should be highly suspicious when, as is common, the same expertise, thinking, technology, and approaches are used for domestic nuclear safeguards as for international nuclear safeguards. Domestic nuclear safeguards is a traditional security application. The bad guys are a small group with limited resources that may try to break in (perhaps with the assistance of insiders) to steal, sabotage or conduct espionage on nuclear material. The resources of the facility can be used to resist the adversary. International safeguards, on the other hand, is treaty monitoring, not regular security *per se*. The adversary is a nation-state with world-class resources available to use in attacks. It owns and controls the nuclear assets of interest and has unlimited access to the facility, which it owns. The attacks can be leisurely. The adversary knows the technical details and must approve all monitoring equipment. In ordinary security, the burglars don't exert substantial control over the burglar alarms!

➤ Be very skeptical of behavioral observation used by TSA, police, or private security personnel to spot likely terrorists or criminals. The effectiveness, science, R&D, metrics, fairness, and rigor are simply not there!

➤ Don't forget that computers, routers, servers, and data centers can be attacked physically and electronically, not just via remote cyber hacking. They can be tampered with in their final end-user location by IT support, other insiders, and outsiders, but also all throughout the supply chain, including at the manufacturer, vendor, or during shipment or while sitting on a loading dock or in a warehouse. This is why a secure chain of custody, starting in the factory, in important.

➤ Routinely check sensitive computers for hardware keystroke recorders and for miniature video transmitters in the room.

➤ Warn employees of likely listening bugs while on foreign travel.

➤ Consider having an innocent sounding but rarely used word or phrase that acts as a panic code word. Employees or security personnel can use the code word

Other Security Tips

verbally or in a text or email say to indicate they are being threatened or are otherwise in distress. The code word for regular employees should be different from that for security personnel.

➢ Beware of computer mono-culture: having just PCs, Macs, Linux, OpenBSD machines, etc.

➢ Don't make your SOC your NOC. Too many conflicts of interest and differing priorities!

➢ Make sure that regular employees know how to identify legitimate IT personnel and instructions. If a thumb drive shows up on their desk or in their mailbox with a memo apparently from IT saying to install this software, will they mindlessly do it?

➢ Use 2-factor authentication.

➢ Be skeptical of using text analytics (monitoring email and text messages) to spy on employees, thus removing an avenue for employee venting and encouraging mistrust. Instead consider periodically reminding employees that texts and emails are forever, and become public when there is litigation.

➢ With Internet of Things (IoT) devices, be sure to change the default passwords, device ID, and security settings. Have a very secure chain of custody for procurement. Be sure the devices follow minimalist principles: no more range, power, duty cycle, bandwidth, or data acquisition/retention/duration than necessary. Be sure IoT devices are included in your overall security plan. Note that IoT devices is one area where newly emerging standards for privacy and security may actually have considerable merit.

➢ Check out the *Journal of Physical Security* at http://jps.rbsekurity.com. It is a free, non-profit, online, (mostly) peer-reviewed journal devoted to physical security, both the technical and social science aspects. Also consider submitting a manuscript for consideration!

I always pass on good advice. It is the only thing to do with it.
It is never of any use to oneself.
-- Oscar Wilde (1854-1900)

Chapter 14 Discussion and Thought Questions

1. Why is layered security dangerous? Why is it nevertheless often needed?

2. How can you make layer security more effective when it is needed, and avoid its pitfalls?

3. How secure is your chain of custody for an access control devices and IT equipment, including computers and routers?

4. What is meant by "a secure chain of custody is not a piece of paper where random people scribble the date and their signature or initials"? What is it then?

5. Are security devices, computers, thumb drives, and routers routinely checked in your organization for physical/electronic tampering, counterfeiting, and hijacking?

6. What IoT devices do you use? Do you and your organization pay enough attention to the security and privacy issues associated with them?

7. How are the challenges and culture of physical security and cyber security different? How are they the same? What do you think they could learn from each other?

8. Why is getting physical and cyber security professionals to work well together—sometimes called the "thugs vs. the nerds problem"—often so challenging? What can make it work better?

9. What are the pros and cons of text analytics?

10. What are behavioral observations dubious for spotting terrorists and criminals? What <u>rigorous</u> scientific research can you find to support or refute behavioral observations?

11. Why is peer review good for security? Does your organization do it?

Appendix – Security Maxims

I like maxims that don't require behavior modification.
-- Calvin from *Calvin and Hobbes*, by Bill Watterson

This is a revised and updated list of my popular security maxims that have popped up in various places through the years. Many are cynical, smart-ass, or tongue-in-cheek, but that does not make them untrue. You ignore these maxims at your own (and others') peril, especially the ones marked with an asterisk!

While these maxims are not theorems or absolute truths, they are in my experience, essentially valid 80-90% of the time in physical security and nuclear safeguards. They probably also have considerable applicability to cyber security.

Most of these are my own invention though some are old adages of unknown origin, at least to me. When somebody else deserves credit, he or she is acknowledged in the name of the maxim or "law", and/or in the comments that follow many of the maxims.

1. Arrogance Maxim: The ease of defeating a security device or system is proportional to how confident/arrogant the designer, manufacturer, or user is about it, and to how often they use words like "impossible" or "tamper-proof".

2. Warner's (Chinese Proverb) Maxim: There is only one beautiful baby in the world, and every mother has it. Comment: Everybody's security or security product is beautiful (to them).

*3. Band-Aid Maxim: Effective security is difficult enough when designed in from scratch. It can rarely be added on at the end, or as an afterthought. Comment: So plan security at the earliest design stages of a security device, system, or program.

4. Get Use To It Maxim: The recommended use protocol for any given security device, system, or product (if there even is one) is not well thought through from a vulnerability standpoint.

*5. Be Afraid, Be Very Afraid Maxim: If you're not running scared, you have bad security or a bad security product. <u>Comment</u>: Fear is a good vaccine against both arrogance and ignorance.

*6. So We're In Agreement Maxim: If you're happy with your security, so are the bad guys.

*7. Ignorance is Bliss Maxim: The confidence that people have in security is inversely proportional to how much they know about it. <u>Comment</u>: Security looks easy if you've never taken the time to think carefully about it.

8. Titanic Maxim: All confidence is over-confidence, if not arrogance.

9. Infinity Maxim: There are an unlimited number of security vulnerabilities for a given security device, system, or program, most of which will never be discovered (by the good guys or bad guys). <u>Comment</u>: We think this is true because we always find new vulnerabilities when we look at the same security device, system, or program a second or third time, and because we always find vulnerabilities that others miss, and vice versa.

10. Thanks for Nothin' Maxim: A vulnerability assessment that finds no vulnerabilities or only a few is worthless and wrong.

11. Weakest Link Maxim: The efficacy of security is determined more by what is done wrong than by what is done right. <u>Comment</u>: Because the bad guys typically attack deliberately and intelligently, not randomly.

12. Safety Maxim: Applying the methods of safety to security doesn't work well, but the reverse may have some merit. <u>Comment</u>: Safety is typically analyzed as a stochastic or event/fault tree kind of problem, whereas the bad guys typically attack deliberately and intelligently, not randomly. For a discussion about using security methods to improve safety, see my proposal in *Journal of Safety Research* **35**, 245-248 (2004).

*13. High-Tech Maxim: The amount of careful thinking that has gone into a given security device, system, or program is inversely proportional to the amount of high-technology it uses. <u>Comment</u>: In security, high-technology is often taken as a license to stop thinking critically.

14. Doctor Who Maxim: "The more sophisticated the technology, the more vulnerable it is to primitive attack. People often overlook the obvious." <u>Comment</u>: This quote is from Tom Baker as Doctor Who in *The Pirate Planet* (1978).

*15. Low-Tech Maxim: Low-tech attacks work (even against high-tech devices and systems). <u>Comment</u>: So don't get too worked up about high-tech attacks.

16. Black Box Maxim: An adversary can defeat a security device or system (even if high-tech) with only a partial understanding of how it (or the software/firmware) works. <u>Comment</u>: Based on a lot of experience.

17. Schneier's Maxim #1 (Don't Wet Your Pants Maxim): The more excited people are about a given security technology, the less they understand (1) that technology and (2) their own security problems. <u>Comment</u>: From security guru Bruce Schneier.

18. Sexy Maxim: The sexier a security device, system, or program appears to be, the less security it has to offer.

19. What a Deal Maxim: The introduction of high-tech security products into your security program will: (1) probably not improve your security, (2) almost certainly increase your overall security costs (though perhaps it will decrease inventory, shipping,

or other business costs), and (3) probably increase security labor costs (with the sometimes exception of CCTV).

20. Too Good Maxim: If a given security product, technology, vendor, or techniques sounds too good to be true, it is. And it probably sucks big time.

*21. You Must Be High Maxim 1: Any security product that is labeled "high security" isn't.

*22. You Must Be High Maxim 2: "High Security" is a context- and application-dependent value judgment, not a product attribute.

23. That's Extra Maxim: Any given security product is unlikely to have significant security built in, and will thus be relatively easy to defeat.

24. I Just Work Here Maxim: No salesperson, engineer, or executive of a company that sells or designs security products or services is prepared to answer a significant question about vulnerabilities, and few potential customers will ever ask them one.

25. Bob Knows a Guy Maxim: Most security products and services will be chosen by the end-user based on purchase price plus hype, rumor, innuendo, hearsay, and gossip.

26. My Crazy Girlfriend/Boyfriend Maxim: Any methodology for selecting a security device or system (or for deciding whether a new one should be fielded) will deliberately ignore, assign insufficient weight to, or be ignorant of the fact that it can be easily defeated. Consequently, the device or system will be accepted for reasons other than effective security. Comment: (Named after people who select a romantic partner with many admirable traits but who happens to be a psychopath.) If a security device or system does not provide good security, any of its other attributes are irrelevant. The maxim applies to qualitative, semi-quantitative, and quantitative methodologies for ranking/rating.

27. He Just Seems So Knowledgeable Maxim: Most organizations get the majority of their physical security advice from salespeople (who somehow seem to recommend their own products), or from colleagues who got their information from salespeople.

28. Tamper-Proof Maxim: Any claim by a salesperson about the performance of a physical security product (including the claim of absolute security) will be believed by default by the customer, while warnings about vulnerabilities or limitations by vulnerability assessors or others with first-hand experience will be met with incredulity. <u>Comment</u>: A classic example of this can be found in the all-to-common seal customers who maintain that the seals they use cannot be spoofed because the manufacturer calls them "tamper-proof".

29. Magic Light Inside the Refrigerator Maxim: Deploying a simple mechanical tamper switch or light sensor to detect tampering with a device (e.g., a motion sensor) or container is approximately the same thing as having no tamper detection at all. <u>Comment</u>: The reasons for this include (1) such tamper detectors are usually easy for a resourceful person to defeat, (2) they are often poorly designed, (3) the tamper signal/alarm is ignored or misinterpreted, and/or (4) the tamper signal is often not even hooked up.

30. Key Maxim (Tobias's Maxim #1): The key does not unlock the lock. <u>Comment</u>: From Marc Weber Tobias. The point is that the key activates a mechanism that unlocks the lock. The bad guys can go directly to that central unlocking mechanism to attack the lock (or do other things) and entirely bypass the key or pins. This maxim is related to the "I am Spartacus Maxim" below and to a corollary (also from Marc Weber Tobias) that "electrons don't open doors, mechanical mechanisms do".

31. Tobias's Maxim #2: Things are rarely what they appear to be. <u>Comment</u>: From Marc Weber Tobias. Or as Yogi Berra said, "Nothing is like it seems, but everything is exactly like it is."

32. There's The Opening Maxim (Tobias's Maxim #3): Any opening in a security product creates a vulnerability. <u>Comment</u>: From Marc Weber Tobias.

33. Tobias's Maxim #4: You must carefully examine both critical and non-critical components to understand security. <u>Comment</u>: From Marc Weber Tobias.

34. Contrived Duelism/Dualism Maxim: The promoters of any security product meant to deal with any sufficiently challenging security problem will invoke a logical fallacy (called "Contrived Dualism") where only 2 alternatives are presented and we are pressured into making a choice, even though there are actually other possibilities. <u>Comment</u>: For example: "We found a convicted felon, gave him a crowbar, and he couldn't make the lock open after whaling on it for 10 minutes. Therefore, the lock is secure." Another example, "Nobody in the company that manufacturers this product can figure out how to defeat it, and I bet you, Mr./Ms. Potential Customer [never having seen this product before in your life] can't think up a viable attack on the spot. Therefore, this product is secure."

35. Familiarity Maxim: Any security technology becomes more vulnerable to attacks when it becomes more widely used, and when it has been used for a longer period of time.

36. Antique Maxim: A security device, system, or program is most vulnerable near the end of its life.

*37. Schneier's Maxim #2 (Control Freaks Maxim): Control will usually get confused with Security. <u>Comment</u>: From security guru Bruce Schneier. Even when Control doesn't get confused with Security, lots of people and organizations will use Security as an excuse to grab Control, e.g., the Patriot Act.

38. Father Knows Best Maxim: The amount that (non-security) senior managers in any organization know about security is inversely proportional to (1) how easy they think security is, and (2) how much they will micro-manage security and invent arbitrary rules.

39. Big Heads Maxim: The farther up the chain of command a (non-security) manager can be found, the more likely he or she thinks that (1) they understand security and (2) security is easy.

40. Huh Maxim: When a (non-security) senior manager, bureaucrat, or government official talks publicly about security, he or she will usually say something stupid, unrealistic, inaccurate, and/or naïve.

41. It's All About Me Maxim: Government employees involved with security and counter intelligence will confuse what makes their job easier with what is good for the nation's security.

*42. Voltaire's Maxim: The problem with common sense is that it is not all that common. Comment: Real world security blunders are often stunningly dumb.

43. Yippee Maxim: There are effective, simple, and low-cost countermeasures (at least partial countermeasures) to most vulnerabilities.

44. Arg Maxim: But users, manufacturers, managers, and bureaucrats will be reluctant to implement them for reasons of inertia, pride, bureaucracy, fear, wishful thinking, and/or cognitive dissonance.

*45. Show Me Maxim: No serious security vulnerability, including blatantly obvious ones, will be dealt with until there is overwhelming evidence and widespread recognition that adversaries have already catastrophically exploited it. In other words, "significant psychological (or literal) damage is required before any significant security changes will be made".

*46. Friedman's Maxim: "Only a crisis—actual or perceived—produces real change. When the crisis occurs, the actions that are taken depend on the ideas that are lying around." --Milton Friedman (1912-2006). Comment: This is why it is so important to actively discuss and analyze alternative approaches to security. Not because they will be automatically adopted even if they are good ideas, but because we want lots of good ideas lying around for when a real or perceived serious security incident occurs.

47. Could've, Would've, Should've Maxim: Organizations and Security Managers will dismiss a serious vulnerability as of no consequence if there exists a simple countermeasure—even if they haven't bothered to actually implement that countermeasure.

48. Payoff Maxim: The more money that can be made from defeating a technology, the more attacks, attackers, and hackers will appear.

49. I Hate You Maxim 1: The more a given technology is despised or distrusted, the more attacks, attackers, and hackers will appear.

50. I Hate You Maxim 2: The more a given technology hassles or annoys security personnel, the less effective it will be.

51. Good vs. Evil Maxim: Ethical hackers improve security more often than they place it at risk.

52. Colsch's (KISS or Kitchen Sink) Maxim: Security won't work if there are too many different security measures to manage, and/or they are too complicated or hard to use.

53. That's Cold Maxim: An adversary who attacks cold (without advance knowledge or preparation) is stupid and amateurish, often too much so to be a real threat. Moreover, he almost never has to attack cold. Comment: Thus, don't overly focus on this kind of attack, or use it as an excuse not to fix vulnerabilities.

54. Shannon's (Kerckhoffs') Maxim: The adversaries know and understand the security hardware, software, algorithms, and strategies being employed. Comment: This is one of the reasons why open source security (e.g., open source software, cryptography, or locks) makes sense.

55. Corollary to Shannon's Maxim: Thus, "Security by Obscurity", i.e., security based on keeping long-term secrets, is not a good idea. Comment: Short-term secrets can create useful uncertainty for an adversary, such as temporary passwords and unpredictable schedules for guard rounds. But relying on long term secrets for good security is not smart. People and organizations cannot keep long-term secrets.

56. Transparency Maxim: Security is usually better when it is transparent. Comment: Ironically—and somewhat counter-intuitively—security is usually more effective when it is transparent. This allows for discussion, analysis, understanding, outside review, criticism, accountability, better metrics, buy-in, and continuing improvement.

57. Gossip Maxim: People and organizations can't keep secrets. Comment: See Manning and Snowden.

58. How Inconvenient! Maxim: Convenience is typically not compatible with good security, yet, paradoxically, security that isn't convenient usually doesn't work well.

*59. Plug into the Formula Maxim: Engineers don't understand security. Comment: They tend to work in solution space, not problem space. They rely on conventional designs and focus on a good experience for the user and manufacturer, rather than a bad experience for the bad guy. They view nature or economics as the adversary, not people, and instinctively think about systems failing stochastically, rather than due to deliberate, intelligent, malicious intent. Being intelligent does not automatically make you think like a bad guy. (Magicians, lawyers, and con artists know that technical people are often the easiest people to scam because they think logically!)

60. Rohrbach's Maxim: No security device, system, or program will ever be used properly (the way it was designed) all the time.

61. Rohrbach Was An Optimist Maxim: No security device, system, or program will ever be used properly.

62. Ox Votes for the Moron Maxim: "Election Security" is an oxymoron.

63. Election Oaf Ficial Maxim: Any given election official most likely (1) doesn't believe that security is part of their job, (2) doesn't think there are any election security issues, (3) has never tried to envision an attack, and (4) believes any questioning of their election security is a political attack.

64. Not My Problem Maxim: The only for-profit organizations more clueless about security than manufacturers and vendors of security products are manufacturers and vendors who make products that they (mistakenly) think have no security implications or potential attackers. Comment: Examples: electronic voting machines and medical electronics.

*65. Security Costs Extra Maxim: You won't usually get better security products by telling the manufacturer or vendor about the vulnerabilities, but you'll have a somewhat better chance if you tell the customers and let the manufacturer/vendor know you have.

66. Thanks But No Thanks Maxim: It is a waste of time to try to help a person or organization improve their security if one or more of the following are true: (1) They are arrogant in denial about their security problems; (2) They don't think their security can improve; (3) They don't want their security to improve; and/or (4) They are pathologically unimaginative or stupid.

67. Purely Reflexive (PR) Maxim: After a public hacking, tampering event, or serious security incident, the lawyers, senior management, and the Public Relations Department will be unprepared and will handle the situation in an incompetent, knee-jerk, self-defeating manner that harms the organization and its reputation.

68. Inside Tip Maxim: There are always real and substantial insider threats.

*69. Insider Risk Maxim: Most organizations will ignore or seriously underestimate the threat from insiders. Comment: Maybe from a combination of denial that we've hired bad people, and a (justifiable) fear of how hard it is to deal with the insider threat?

*70. We Have Met the Enemy and He is Us Maxim: The insider threat from careless or complacent employees and contractors exceeds the threat from malicious insiders (though the latter is not negligible.) Comment: This is partially, though not totally, due to the fact that careless or complacent insiders often unintentionally help nefarious outsiders. Also, see Schryver's Law below.

71. Fair Thee Well Maxim: Employers who talk a lot about treating employees fairly typically treat employees neither fairly nor (more importantly) well, thus aggravating the insider threat and employee turnover (which is also bad for security).

72. The Inmates are Happy Maxim: Large organizations and senior managers will go to great lengths to deny employee disgruntlement, see it as an insider threat, or do anything about it. Comment: There are a wide range of well-established tools for mitigating disgruntlement. Most are quite inexpensive.

73. Two Kinds Maxim 1: Disengaged employees fall into 2 categories, those who quit and leave, and those who quit and stay.

74. Two Kinds Maxim 2: Disgruntled employees fall into 2 categories, those who engage in retaliation and sabotage, and those who are currently contemplating it.

75. Beef Jerky Maxim: Employees don't leave jobs, they leave jerks.

*76. Make 'Em Gruntled Maxim: Disgruntlement is the easiest motivator of inside attackers to counter. Comment: There are a number of motivations for deliberate inside attacks. These include: greed; ideology, political activism, and radicalization; terrorism; coercion/blackmail; desire for excitement; the phenomenon of a self-identified Cassandra; disgruntlement; and (maybe) mental illness. Of these, disgruntlement is the easiest to counter by treating insiders well, followed by dealing with Cassandras. [In Greek mythology, Cassandra was given the power of prophecy, but then cursed such that nobody would believe her. A self-identified Cassandra warns of security risks, but when isn't believed will instigate the prophesized attack(s).]

77. 80% Maxim: When an employee is disgruntled, if someone in the organization with even a little authority will simply listen to, validate, and empathize with the employee, approximately 80% of the time the employee will feel significantly better about the problem, himself/herself, and the organization as a whole. Comment: Remarkably, it isn't even necessary to agree with the employee about their complaint(s), or fix whatever is bugging him or her—though, when possible, a sincere attempt to fix the problem can go a long ways towards mitigating the disgruntlement.

78. HR Maxim: In any given large organization, the Human Resources Department is more likely to make security worse than it is to make it better. Indeed, your greatest security threat may be HR.

*79. Troublemaker Maxim: The probability that a security professional has been marginalized by his or her organization is proportional to his/her skill, creativity, knowledge, competence, and eagerness to provide effective security.

80. Feynman's Maxim: An organization will fear and despise loyal vulnerability assessors and others who point out vulnerabilities or suggest security changes more than malicious adversaries. Comment: An entertaining example of this common phenomenon can be found in the book, *Surely You are Joking, Mr. Feynman!*, published by W.W. Norton, 1997. During the Manhattan Project, when physicist Richard Feynman pointed out physical security vulnerabilities, he was banned from the facility, rather than having the vulnerability dealt with (which would have been easy).

*81. Questionable Security Maxim: If nobody is questioning or criticizing your security, you have bad security.

82. Irresponsibility Maxim: It'll often be considered "irresponsible" to point out security vulnerabilities (including the theoretical possibility that they might exist), but you'll rarely be called irresponsible for ignoring or covering them up.

*83. Backwards Maxim: Most people will assume everything is secure until provided strong evidence to the contrary—exactly backwards from a reasonable approach.

84. Narcissist Maxim: Security managers, bureaucrats, manufacturers, vendors, and end-users will automatically assume that, if they cannot readily conceive of a way to defeat a security product (or a security program), then nobody else can. Remarkably, this will be true even for people with little or no experience, resources, or aptitude for defeating security, and even if they are spectacularly unimaginative or stupid.

85. You Could've Knocked Me Over with a Feather Maxim 1: Security managers, bureaucrats, manufacturers, vendors, and end-users will always be amazed at how easily their security products or programs can be defeated.

86. You Could've Knocked Me Over with a Feather Maxim 2: Having been amazed once, security managers, bureaucrats, manufacturers, vendors, and end-users will be equally amazed the next time around.

87. That's Why They Pay Us the Big Bucks Maxim: Security is nigh near impossible. It's extremely difficult to stop a determined adversary. Often the best you can do is discourage him, and maybe minimize the consequences when he does attack, and/or maximize your organization's ability to bounce back (resiliency).

88. Throw the Bums Out Maxim: An organization that fires high-level security managers when there is a major security incident, or severely disciplines or fires low-level security personnel when there is a minor incident, will never have good security.

*89. Scapegoat Maxim: The main purpose of an official inquiry after a serious security incident is to find somebody to blame, not to fix the problems.

90. Eeny, Meeny, Miny Maxim: The scapegoat(s) chosen after a serious security incident will tend to be chosen from among these 3 groups: those who had nothing to do with the incident, those who lacked the authority and resources to prevent it, and those whose warnings about the possibility of this or related incidents went unheeded.

91. A Priest, a Minister, and a Rabbi Maxim: People lacking imagination, skepticism, and a sense of humor should not work in the security field.

92. I Question This Maxim Maxim: Skepticism about security (if not all-out cynicism) is almost always warranted. Moreover, it is a powerful tool for analyzing or evaluating security.

93. Thinking Outside the Bun Maxim: Any security manager who cannot think of a new place to have lunch oversees a poor security program.

*94. Absence of Evidence As Evidence of Absence Maxim: The fact that any given unimaginative bureaucrat or security manager cannot immediately envision a viable attack scenario will be taken as proof that there are no vulnerabilities.

95. That's Not My Department Maxim: Any employee who's job primarily entails checking on security compliance will have no interest in (or understanding of) security, will not permit it to interfere with his/her job, and will look at you like you are crazy if you raise any actual security concerns.

96. Deer in the Headlights (I'm With Stupid) Maxim: Any sufficiently advanced cowardice, fear, arrogance, denial, ignorance, laziness, or bureaucratic intransigence is indistinguishable from stupidity.

*97. Cowboy Maxim: You can lead a jackass to security, but you can't make him think.

Vulnerability Assessment

98. Awareness Training: Most security awareness training turns employees against security and/or hypocritically represents the organization as having a good Security Culture when it does not.

99. See I (Just Work Here) Maxim 1: (Your security awareness or CI training not withstanding) any given Counter-Intelligence (CI) Officer doesn't want to hear about your CI concerns, and will do nothing about them if they are forced upon him/her.

100. See I (Just Work Here) Maxim 2: Any bureaucrat sufficiently high up in the Security or Counter-Intelligence Department doesn't get Counter Intelligence (CI).

*101. Mr. Spock Maxim: The effectiveness of a security device, system, or program is inversely proportional to how angry or upset people get about the idea that there might be vulnerabilities.

102. Double Edge Sword Maxim: Within a few months of its availability, new technology helps the bad guys at least as much as it helps the good guys.

*103. Mission Creep Maxim: Any given device, system, or program that is designed for inventory will very quickly come to be viewed—quite incorrectly—as a security device, system, or program. <u>Comment</u>: This is a sure recipe for lousy security. Examples include RFIDs, GPS, and many so-called nuclear Material Control and Accountability (MC&A) programs.

*104. We'll Worry About it Later Maxim: Effective security is difficult enough when you design it in from first principles. It almost never works to retrofit it in, or to slap security on at the last minute, especially onto inventory technology.

*105. Somebody Must've Thought It Through Maxim: The more important the security application, the less careful and critical thought and research has gone into it. <u>Comment</u>: Research-based practice is rare in important security applications. For example, while the security of candy and soda vending machines has been carefully analyzed and researched, the security of nuclear materials has not. Perhaps this is because when we have a very important security application, committees, bureaucrats, power grabbers, business managers, and linear/plodding/unimaginative thinkers take over. Also, there is mental paralysis because the stakes are so high.

106. That's Entertainment Maxim: Ceremonial Security (a.k.a. "Security Theater") will usually be confused with Real Security; even when it is not, it will be favored over Real Security. Comment: Thus, after September 11, airport screeners confiscated passengers' fingernail clippers, apparently under the theory that a hijacker might threaten the pilot with a bad manicure. At the same time, there was no significant screening of the cargo and luggage loaded onto passenger airplanes.

107. Ass Sets Maxim: Most security programs focus on protecting the wrong assets. Comment: Often the focus is excessively on physical assets, not more important assets such as people, intellectual property, trade secrets, good will, an organization's reputation, customer and vendor privacy, etc.

*108. Vulnerabilities Trump Threats Maxim: If you know your vulnerabilities (weaknesses) and have dealt with them, you may be ok even if you are confused on the threats. But if you focus only on the threats, you're likely to be in trouble by not understanding your vulnerabilities and the possible attack scenarios. Comment: It's hard to predict the threats accurately, but threats (real or imagined) are great for scaring an organization into action. It's actually not so hard to find the vulnerabilities if you really want to, but it can be difficult to get anybody to do anything about them.

109. Vulnerabilities are the Threat Maxim: Security (and emergency response) typically fails not because the threats were misunderstood, but because the vulnerabilities were not recognized and/or not mitigated.

110. See No Evil Maxim: Organizations and security managers are more afraid of vulnerabilities than threats, so much so that they will often deny that vulnerabilities can exist, rather than address them.

111. Gap Maxim: People and organizations that talk about "gaps" in their security (rather than vulnerabilities or attack scenarios) have middling security at best. <u>Comment</u>: At least they are able to acknowledge that vulnerabilities can exist (a good thing) but the gap/no-gap binary mindset is not conducive to good security.

112. Risky Business Maxim: Many of the activities involved in developing or evaluating security measures will only have a partial or superficial connection to true Risk Management.

113. Stupid Met Tricks Maxim: Any given security metric is more likely to measure security management, compliance with rules, or performance against one very specific (and improbable) attack scenario than actual security. And it probably drives more undesirable security behaviors and attitudes than good ones.

114. Mermaid Maxim: The most common excuse for not fixing security vulnerabilities is the belief that they simply can't exist. <u>Comment</u>: Often, the evidence offered that no security vulnerabilities exist is that the security manager who expresses this view can't personally imagine how to defeat the security.

115. Onion Maxim: The second most common excuse for not fixing security vulnerabilities is that "we have many layers of security", i.e., we rely on "Security in Depth". <u>Comment</u>: Layered security has its uses, but it should not be the knee jerk response to difficult security challenges, nor an excuse to stop thinking and improving security, as it often is.

116. Hopeless Maxim: The third most common excuse for not fixing security vulnerabilities is that "all security devices, systems, and programs can be defeated". <u>Comment</u>: This maxim is typically expressed by the same person who initially invoked the Mermaid Maxim, when he/she is forced to acknowledge that the vulnerabilities actually exist because they've been demonstrated in his/her face. A common variant of the Hopeless Maxim is "Sure, we could implement that inexpensive countermeasure so that the average person on the street couldn't defeat our security

with a bobby pin, but then the bad guys would just come up with another, more sophisticated attack".

117. Takes One to Know One Maxim: The fourth most common excuse for not fixing security vulnerabilities is that "our adversaries are too stupid and/or unresourceful to figure that out." <u>Comment</u>: Never underestimate your adversaries, or the extent to which people will go to defeat security. Adversaries can always hire or exploit brains, skills, and creative people.

118. Depth, What Depth? Maxim: For any given security program, the amount of critical, skeptical, creative, and intelligent thinking that has been undertaken is inversely proportional to how strongly the strategy of "Security in Depth" (layered security) is embraced.

*119. Waylayered Security Maxim: Complex layered security will fail stupidly. <u>Comment</u>: See, for example, the 82-year old nun penetrating the Y-12 nuclear facility, or various White House fence jumpers over the years.

120. Gatekeeper ("We'll Only Get Suspicious When Bob Does") Maxim: Organizations and security managers will frequently deploy multiple security measures (perhaps layered), but only put them into play if a particular measure (or layer) indicates there might be a problem—thus largely negating the other measures (or layers). Thus, adversaries often need to spoof or neutralize only one key measure to defeat the overall security. <u>Comment</u>: The 1 security measure (or layer) that is relied upon is usually the easiest to interrupt. Examples of this maxim: (1) In some facilities, guards do nothing until an audible alarm sounds. (2) If a cargo tamper-indicating seal appears intact, it may not be carefully inspected or its serial number compared with records—thus ignoring most of its relevant security.

121. Redundancy/Orthogonality Maxim: When different security measures are thought of as redundant or "backups", they typically are not. <u>Comment</u>: Redundancy is often mistakenly assumed because the disparate functions of the two security measures aren't carefully thought through.

122. Tabor's Maxim #1 (Narcissism Maxim): Security is an illusionary ideal created by people who have an overvalued sense of their own self worth. <u>Comment</u>: From Derek Tabor. This maxim is cynical even by my depressing standards—though that doesn't make it wrong.

123. Tabor's Maxim #2 (Cost Maxim): Security is practically achieved by making the cost of obtaining or damaging an asset higher than the value of the asset itself. <u>Comment</u>: From Derek Tabor. Note that "cost" isn't necessarily measured in terms of dollars.

124. Buffett's Maxim: You should only use security hardware, software, and strategies you understand. <u>Comment</u>: This is analogous to Warren Buffett's advice on how to invest, but it applies equally well to security. While it's little more than common sense, this advice is routinely ignored by security managers.

*125. Just Walk It Off Maxim: Most organizations will become so focused on prevention (which is very difficult at best), that they fail to adequately plan for mitigating attacks, and for recovering when attacks inevitably occur.

126. Thursday Maxim: Organizations and security managers will tend to automatically invoke irrational or fanciful reasons for claiming that they are immune to any postulated or demonstrated attack. <u>Comment</u>: So named because if the attack or vulnerability was demonstrated on a Tuesday, it won't be viewed as applicable on Thursday. My favorite example of this maxim is when we made a video showing how to use GPS spoofing to hijack a truck that uses GPS tracking. In that video, the GPS antenna was shown attached to the side of the truck so that it could be easily seen on the video. After viewing the video, one security manager said it was all very interesting, but not relevant for their operations because their trucks had the antenna on the roof.

127. Galileo's Maxim: The more important the assets being guarded, or the more vulnerable the security program, the less willing its security managers will be to hear about vulnerabilities. <u>Comment</u>: The name of this maxim comes from the 1633

Inquisition where Church officials refused to look into Galileo's telescope out of fear of what they might see.

*128. Michener's Maxim: We are never prepared for what we expect. <u>Comment</u>: From a quote by author James Michener (1907-1997). As an example, consider Hurricane Katrina or the Covid-19 pandemic.

129. Black Ops Maxim: If facility security is the responsibility of the Facility Management or (in government) Operations Department, then security will be given about as much importance and careful analysis as snow removal or picking up the trash.

130. Accountability 1 Maxim: Organizations that talk a lot about holding people accountable for security are talking about mindless retaliation, not a sophisticated approach to motivating good security practices by trying to understand human and organizational psychology, and the realities of the workplace.

131. Accountability 2 Maxim: Organizations that talk a lot about holding people accountable for security will never have good security. <u>Comment</u>: Because if all you can do is threaten people, rather than developing and motivating good security practices, you will not get good results in the long term.

132. Ogburn's (Blind-Sided) Maxim: Organizations will usually be totally unprepared for the security implications of new technology, and the first impulse will be to try to mindlessly ban it. <u>Comment</u>: Thus increasing the cynicism regular (non-security) employees have about security.

133. Better to be Lucky than Good Maxim: Most of the time when security appears to be working, it's because no adversary is currently prepared to attack.

134. Success Maxim: Most security programs "succeed" (in the sense of their being no apparent major security incidents) not on their merits but for one of these reasons: (1) the attack was surreptitious and has not yet been detected, (2) the attack was

covered up by insiders afraid of retaliation and is not yet widely known, (3) the bad guys are currently inept but that will change, or (4) there are currently no bad guys interested in exploiting the vulnerabilities, either because other targets are more tempting or because bad guys are actually fairly rare.

135. Rigormortis Maxim: The greater the amount of rigor claimed or implied for a given security analysis, vulnerability assessment, risk management exercise, or security design, the less careful, clever, critical, imaginative, and realistic thought has gone into it.

136. Catastrophic Maxim: Most organizations mistakenly think about and prepare for rare, catastrophic attacks (if they do so at all) in the same way as for minor security incidents.

137. I am Spartacus Maxim: Most vulnerability or risk assessments will let the good guys (and the existing security infrastructure, hardware, and strategies) define the problem, in contrast to real-world security applications where the bad guys get to. Comment: Named for the catch-phrase from the 1960 Stanley Kubrick film *Spartacus*. When the Romans captured Spartacus' army, they demanded he identify himself, but all his soldiers claimed to be Spartacus. Not historically accurate, but very Hollywood!

138. Methodist Maxim: While vulnerabilities determine the methods of attack, most vulnerability or risk assessments will act as if the reverse were true.

139. Tucker's Maxim #1 (Early Bird & Worm Maxim): An adversary is most vulnerable to detection and disruption just prior to an attack. Comment: So seize the initiative in the adversary's planning stages. From Craig Tucker.

140. Tucker's Maxim #2 (Toss the Dice Maxim): When the bullets start flying, it's a crapshoot and nobody can be sure how it'll turn out. Comment: So don't let it get to that point. From Craig Tucker.

141. Tucker's Maxim #3 (Failure = Success Maxim): If you're not failing when you're training or testing your security, you're not learning anything. <u>Comment</u>: From Craig Tucker.

142. Gunslingers' Maxim: Any government security program will mistakenly focus more on dealing with force-on-force attacks and brute force methods than on more likely attacks involving insider threats and subtle, surreptitious approaches.

143. We Built This Door for You: The security of most facilities will be based on the wrong idea that the bad guys will use the existing doors, stairs, and hallways to execute an attack. <u>Comment</u>: And security sensors, video cameras, and guards will be hopelessly misplaced as a result.

144. Fool-On-Fool Maxim: The incompetence of any security program is proportional to the degree of obsession with idea that the major threat is a small band of stupid, unprepared adversaries who mindlessly attack straight on, using force and zero insiders. <u>Comment</u>: Somehow, the number of envisioned attackers is always less or equal to than the number the security program can purportedly neutralize.

*145. 3D Maxim: The incompetence of any security program is proportional to how strongly the mantra of "Deter, Detect, Delay" is embraced. <u>Comment</u>: This philosophy, while theoretically having some merit, is (as a practical matter) strongly correlated with unimaginative, non-proactive security.

146. D(OU)BT Maxim: If you think Design Basis Threat (DBT) is something to test your security against, then you don't understand DBT and you don't understand your security application. <u>Comment</u>: If done properly—which it often is not—DBT is for purposes of allocating security resources based on probabilistic analyses, not judging security effectiveness. Moreover, if the threat probabilities in the DBT analysis are all essentially 1, which is common, the analysis is deeply flawed.

147. It's Too Quiet Maxim: "Bad guys attack, and good guys react" is not a viable security strategy. <u>Comment</u>: It is necessary to be both proactive in defense, and to preemptively undermine the bad guys in offense.

148. Executive Protection / Peter Principle / Power Corrupts Maxim: Massive resources spent on protecting high-level executives is wasted, as the organization would be much better off without the arrogant, narcissistic, misogynistic, incompetent morons.

149. Nietzsche's Maxim: It's not winning if the good guys have to adopt the unenlightened, illegal, or morally reprehensible tactics of the bad guys. <u>Comment</u>: "Whoever fights monsters should see to it that in the process he does not become a monster." Friedrich Nietzsche (1844-1900), in *Beyond Good and Evil*.

*150. Patton's Maxim: When everybody is thinking alike about security, then nobody is thinking. <u>Comment</u>: Adapted from a broader maxim by General George S. Patton (1885-1945).

151. Kafka's Maxim: The people who write security rules and regulations don't understand (1) what they are doing, or (2) how their policies drive actual security behaviors and misbehaviors.

*152. 30% Maxim: In any large organization, at least 30% of the security rules, policies, and procedures are Security Theater, pointless, absurd, ineffective, naïve, out of date, wasteful, distracting, one-size-fits-all nonsense, or they may even actively undermine security (by creating cynicism about security, ignoring local conditions, or driving bad behaviors that were not anticipated).

153. The Politics Maxim: All security is local. <u>Comment</u>: Security depends on the local, on-the-ground conditions, not on high-level idealized plans for security. <u>Comment</u>: Just like all politics is local, all security is local. The on-the-ground details matter.

154. By the Book Maxim: Full compliance with security rules and regulations is not compatible with optimal security. <u>Comment</u>: Because security rules and regulations are typically dumb and unrealistic (at least partially). Moreover, they often lead to over-confidence, waste time and resources, create unhelpful distractions, engender cynicism about security, and encourage employees to find workarounds to get their job done—thus making security an "us vs. them" game.

*155. Pink Teaming Maxim: Most so-called "vulnerability assessments" are actually threat assessments, compliance auditing, "Red Teaming", penetration testing, or some other exercise (like security surveys, safety analysis, feature analysis, design basis threat, or performance/reliability testing) not well designed to uncover a wide range of security vulnerabilities. <u>Comment</u>: This is much more the case in physical security than in cyber security. Originally, "Red Teaming" meant doing a vulnerability assessment, but it recent years, it has come to mean a one-off, often rigged "test" of a particular, narrowly-defined attack scenario. This may have some value, but is not the same thing as a comprehensive vulnerability assessment looking at a wide range of vulnerabilities and attack scenarios. (For compliance auditing, it is important to remember the 30% Maxim. See above.)

*156. It's About More Than Semantics Maxim: Organizations and security managers that misuse (or don't use at all) the terms "vulnerabilities" or "vulnerability assessments" don't do vulnerability assessments. <u>Comment</u>: While semantics aren't very interesting, language <u>does</u> affect thinking.

*157. Aw Ditz Maxim: Mindlessly auditing if bureaucratic security rules are being followed will usually get confused with a meaningful security review, or a vulnerability assessment. <u>Comment</u>: Compliance-based security doesn't really work. See the 30% Maxim above.

158. Seeing Red Maxim: "Red Teaming" or penetration testing will usually get confused with a comprehensive security review, or a vulnerability assessment.

159. Rig the Rig Maxim: Any supposedly "realistic" test of security is rigged.

160. Cyborg Maxim: Organizations and managers who automatically think "cyber", "IT", "network", or "computer" when somebody says "security", don't have good security (including good cyber security).

161. Caffeine Maxim: On a day-to-day basis, security is mostly about paying attention.

162. Any Donuts Left? Maxim: But paying attention is very difficult.

163. Wolfe's Maxim: If you don't find it often, you often don't find it. <u>Comment</u>: Perceptual blindness and change blindness are huge problems for security officers.

*164. Uncomfortable Truth Maxim: You can be comfortable or you can have good security, but you cannot have both.

165. He Who's Name Must Never Be Spoken Maxim: Security programs and professionals who don't talk a lot about "the adversary" or the "bad guys" or "hackers" or "attackers" aren't prepared for them and don't have good security. <u>Comment</u>: From Harry Potter.

*166. Mahbubani's Maxim: Organizations and security managers who cannot envision security failures, will not be able to avoid them. <u>Comment</u>: Named for scholar and diplomat Kishore Mahbubani. He meant to apply this general principle to politics, diplomacy, and public policy, but it is also applicable to security.

*167. Pen Testing Maxim: You can't test an attack you haven't envisioned. <u>Comment</u>: Thus the importance of vulnerability assessments (not activities that get confused with vulnerability assessments).

168. Hats & Sunglasses Off in the Bank Maxim: Security rules that only the good guys follow are probably Security Theater.

169. Merton's Maxim: The bad guys don't obey our security policies. <u>Comment</u>: This maxim is courtesy of Kevin Sweere. It is named after Thomas Merton (1915-1968), a theological writer and philosopher.

170. Sweere's Maxim (Merton's Corollary): It's worse than that. The bad guys will analyze our security policies and regulations to find exploitable vulnerabilities, including those not envisioned by the good guys.

171. Wall Street Maxim: Every good idea is eventually a bad idea.

172. Dumbestic Safeguards Maxim: Domestic Nuclear Safeguards will inevitably get confused with International Nuclear Safeguards (treaty monitoring), including by people and organizations claiming to fully appreciate that the two applications are very different. <u>Comment</u>: Domestic Nuclear Safeguards is a typical security application—just for very important assets. With International Nuclear Safeguards, in contrast, the bad guys own the assets and facilities of interest, and they fully understand the surveillance, monitoring, and safeguards equipment being used (and may even build, control, and/or install it). It is especially common to overlook or ignore the fact that the adversary in International Nuclear Safeguards is a country, with national- to world-class resources available to defeat the safeguards. [Note: It's sometimes misleading called "International Nuclear Safeguards" when one country or organization, or group of countries try to help a nation improve its own domestic nuclear safeguards, but this is still just Domestic Nuclear Safeguards for the country of interest.]

173. Werther's Maxim: The security of encrypted (or digitally authenticated) information has less to do with the sophistication of the cipher than with the competence, intelligence, diligence, and loyalty of the people who handle it. <u>Comment</u>: From a quote by Waldemar Werther that, "The security of a cipher lies less with the cleverness of the inventor than with the stupidity of the men who are using it."

174. Tobias's Maxim #5: Encryption is largely irrelevant. <u>Comment</u>: From Marc Weber Tobias.

175. Red Herring Maxim: At some point in any challenging security application, somebody (or nearly everybody) will propose or deploy more or less pointless encryption, hashes, digital signatures, or other data authentication along with the often incorrect and largely irrelevant statement that "the cipher [or hash or authentication algorithm] cannot be broken".

Comment: For many security applications where counterfeiting is an issue (like tags and seals), people forget that it's no more difficult to copy encrypted data than it is to copy unencrypted data.

Product anti-counterfeiting tags and International Nuclear Safeguards are two security applications highly susceptible to fuzzy thinking about encryption and data authentication.

With anti-counterfeiting tags, it is no harder for the product counterfeiters to make copies of encrypted data than it is to make copies of unencrypted data. They don't have to understand the encryption scheme or the encrypted data to copy it, so that the degree of difficulty in breaking the encryption (usually overstated) is irrelevant. Indeed, if there was a technology that could preventing cloning of encrypted data (or hashes or digital authentication), then that same technology could be used to prevent cloning of the unencrypted original data, in which case the encryption has no significant role to play. (Sometimes one might wish to send secure information to inspectors who hunt counterfeits in the field, but the security features and encryption typically employed on cell phones or computers is good enough.)

What makes no sense is putting encrypted data on a product, with or without it including encrypted data about an attached anti-counterfeiting tag; the bad guys can easily clone the encrypted data without having to understand it. When there is an anti-counterfeiting tag on a product, only the degree of difficulty of cloning, counterfeiting it, or lifting it is relevant, not the encryption scheme. The use of unique, one-of-a-kind tags (i.e., complexity tags) does not alter the relative unimportance of the encryption as an anti-counterfeiting measure.

Sometimes people promoting encryption for product anti-counterfeiting vaguely have in mind an overly complicated (and usually incomplete/flawed) form of a virtual numeric token ("call-back strategy").   ([See "An Anti-Counterfeiting Strategy Using Numeric Tokens", *International Journal of Pharmaceutical Medicine* **19**, 163-171 (2005).]

Encryption is also often thought of as a silver bullet for International Nuclear Safeguards, partially for reasons given in the Dumbestic Safeguards Maxim. The fact is that encryption or data authentication is of little security value if the adversary can easily break into the equipment holding the secret key without detection (as is usually the case), if there is a serious insider threat that puts the secret encryption key at risk (which is pretty much always the case), and/or if the surveillance or monitoring equipment containing the secret key is designed, controlled, inspected, maintained, stored, observed, or operated by the adversary (as is typically the case in International Nuclear Safeguards).

*176. Anti-Silver Bullet Maxim: If you have poor security before you deploy encryption, digital signatures, or data authentication, you will have poor security after.
Comment: Sometimes, you'll have worse security because the encryption/authentication provides a false sense of security, or causes distractions.

177. It's Standard Maxim: As a general rule of thumb, about two-thirds of security "standards" or "certifications" (though not "guidelines") make security worse.

178. Alice Springs Maxim: Organizations will be loathe to factor in local, on-the-ground details in deciding what security resources to assign to a given location or asset. One-size-fits-all will be greatly preferred because it requires less thinking.
Comment: This maxim is named after the standard reassurance given to worried tourists in Australia that "there aren't a lot of shark attacks in Alice Springs".

179. Follow the Money Maxim: Security attention and resources will usually be doled out in proportion to the absolute dollar value of the assets being protected, not (as it should be) in proportion to the risk.

180. Oh, the Lovely Colors! Maxim: High-level corporate executives will be convinced the organization has good security if they are shown lots of detailed, colorful graphs, Gantt charts, spreadsheets, and calendars concerning security policies, planning, documentation, and training.

181. The MBA Maxim: At high levels in an organization, lots of detailed work on security policies, planning, documentation, scheduling, and charts/graphs/spreadsheets will be preferred over actually thinking carefully and critically about security, or asking critical questions.

182. Fallacy of Precision Maxim 1: If security managers or bureaucrats assign a number or a ranking to some aspect of security (e.g., probability of attack, economic consequences of the loss of an asset, etc.) they will incorrectly think they really understand that aspect and the related security issues.

183. Fallacy of Precision Maxim 2: If there are n bits in the attribute measurement of a given object, then security end-users can be easily (wrongly) convinced that 2^{-n} is: (1) the probability that a similar object matches this one, and/or (2) the probability that somebody can fool the attribute reader, including by "counterfeiting" or mimicking the object so that it has essentially the same attribute measurement. <u>Comment</u>: End-users of security products (especially biometrics or tag readers) will often be fooled by this fallacy. Why is it a fallacy? Among other reasons: Because the bits are not uncorrelated, because they don't all have relevance to the security or authenticity problem (maybe none of them do!), because the degree of correlation between similar objects has not been inputted into the problem, because the type 1 and type 2 errors and tradeoffs haven't been carefully measured or analyzed, because the ease or difficulty of counterfeiting involves many outside factors not factored in, and because the ease or difficulty of otherwise spoofing/hijacking the reader has not been considered.

*184. Apples and Oranges Maxim: Anyone trying to sell you a counterfeit detector, will make a big show of how different objects have different signatures (attribute measurements), but will ignore, oversimplify, or misrepresent the far more important question of how hard it is to fool or tamper with the reader, including by "counterfeiting" or mimicking the object so that it has essentially the same signature. <u>Comment</u>: Manufacturers, vendors, and promoters of biometrics products and tag readers are very fond of doing this.

185. I Second That Motion Maxim: "Security by Committee" is an oxymoron.

186. Nuke that Idea Maxim: Nuclear Security/Safeguards is an oxymoron.

187. Security By Design Maxim: Most security products, facilities, or programs that were designed using so-called "security by design" methods don't actually have much security in them, but at least the word "security" came up early in discussions.

188. Lunkhead Maxim: Lunkheads will be attracted to security management and security supervisory roles, including because their ignorance and incompetence will only be occasionally noted.

189. Fox in the Hen House Maxim: The people selling, installing, and maintaining your security systems are not trustworthy.

190. Any Questions? Maxim: The profundity and novelty of a given security talk is inversely proportional to how many questions are asked by the audience.

191. But Wait! Maxim: Any given security talk is a sales pitch.

192. Let's Get Physical (Security) Maxim: Physical Security is more difficult than Cyber Security (though Cyber Security is plenty hard.) <u>Comment</u>: Cyber Security involves protecting 1's and 0's. Physical security often involves protecting many tangible and intangible assets spread out in time and space, with many possible attack vectors.

193. Reality TV Maxim: Video surveillance does not prevent crime (though it may be useful for documenting crime).

194. Hi Mom! Maxim: When officials release a photo or video recording of a crime, asking if the public recognizes the perpetrator(s), the image quality will be so poor that you couldn't recognize your own mother. <u>Comment</u>: Nowadays, it is malpractice not

to have full resolution HD video images and video recording given the relatively low cost.

195. Squabble Away Maxim: Any security program that lacks open disagreement and discussion about how to proceed with security has lousy security. <u>Comment</u>: Research shows that groups with frequent disagreements (within reason) perform better and are able to solve problems better. This may be because disagreements help to reduce groupthink. It may also be because group members have to actually think through and justify their positions to other group members, resulting in more critical thinking and better ultimate decisions.

The following are general "laws" and "principles" that also apply to security:

196. Fudd's Law: If you push on something hard enough, it will fall over.

197. Hellrung's Law: If you wait long enough, it will go away.

198. Grelb's Law: But if it was bad, it will come back.

*199. Tacitus's Law: To show resentment at a reproach is to acknowledge that one may have deserved it. <u>Comment</u>:: From Tacitus (55-117 AD).

200. Brien's First Law: At some time in the life cycle of virtually every organization, its ability to succeed in spite of itself runs out.

201. Bucy's Law: Nothing is ever accomplished by a reasonable person.

202. Stewart's Law: It is easier to get forgiveness than permission.

203. Horngren's Law: The Real World is a special case.

*204. Glazer's Law: If it's "one size fits all", then it doesn't fit anybody.

205. Gold's Law: If the shoe fits, it's ugly.

206. Firestone's Law: Chicken Little only has to be right once.

207. Shaw's Law: Build a system that even a fool can use, and only a fool will want to use it.

208. Byrne's Law: In any electrical circuit, appliances and wiring will burn out to protect the fuses.

209. Ginsberg's Laws from the beat poet Allen Ginsberg (1926-1997):
The First Law of Thermodynamics: "You can't win."
The Second Law of Thermodynamics: "You can't break even."
The Third Law of Thermodynamics: "You can't quit."

210. Putt's Law: Technology is dominated by two types of people: those who understand what they do not manage, and those who manage what they do not understand.

211. Clarke's First Law: When a distinguished but elderly scientist states that something is possible, he is almost certainly right. When he states that something is impossible, he is probably wrong.

212. Hawkin's Law: Progress does not consist of replacing a theory that is wrong with one that is right. It consists of replacing a theory that is wrong with one that is more subtly wrong.

213. Dunning-Kruger Effect: Incompetent people don't recognize that they are incompetent.

Vulnerability Assessment

214. Sallinger's Law: All morons hate it when you call them a moron. <u>Comment</u>: From J.D. Sallinger (1919-2010).

215. Kernighan's Law: Debugging is twice as hard as writing the software in the first place. Therefore, if you write the software as cleverly as possible, you are (by definition) not smart enough to debug it.

216. Life Cycle of a Good Idea Law: If you have a good idea: first they ignore you, then they ridicule you, then they claim to have thought of it first, then it's declared to be obvious.

217. Not Invented Here Law: If it wasn't invented here, it's a bad idea (unless we can steal the idea and make it look like we thought of it first).

218. Aiken's Law: Don't worry about people stealing your ideas. If your ideas are any good, you'll have to ram them down their throats.

219. Glass Houses Law: The people most obsessed with the work quality of others will typically be among the most incompetent, deadwood screw-ups in the whole organization.

220. Consistent Law: Consistency is the hallmark of small minds and/or bureaucrats, and will routinely get confused with quality.

*221. Peer's Law: The solution to the problem changes the problem. <u>Comment</u>: This is why after implemented changes recommended by a vulnerability or threat assessment, you'll need to re-examine your security.

222. Peter Principle: In a hierarchy, every employee tends to rise to their natural level of incompetence. <u>Comment</u>: From Laurence J. Peter and his 1968 book, *The Peter Principle*. The idea is that employees who do a good job get promoted until they reach a level where they don't do a good job and don't get further promoted. Employees are

loath to turn down a promotion even when they realize they are unqualified or unsuited for it.

223. Peter Principle Corollary: Given enough time, any organization will be dominated by incompetent employees.

224. Orwell's Principle: Being sloppy with security terminology leads to sloppy security thinking and practice. <u>Comment</u>: From this quote by George Orwell (1903-1950): "The slovenliness of our language makes it easier for us to have foolish thoughts." A common example is confusing (or hijacking) the meaning of "vulnerabilities" and "vulnerability assessments" so that effective thinking about vulnerabilities is difficult to do.

225. First Law of Revision: Information necessitating a change of design will be conveyed to the designers after—and only after—the plans are complete.

*226. Grey's/Schryver's Law: Any sufficiently advanced incompetence is indistinguishable from malice. <u>Comment</u>: Security incompetence is very much an insider threat.

About the Author

Roger G. Johnston, Ph.D., CPP received his bachelor's degree from Carleton College, and M.S. and Ph.D. degrees in physics from the University of Colorado. He has won numerous awards, received 10 U.S. patents, authored over 200 papers and book chapters, and has given more than 100 invited talks in 10 countries. In his spare time, Dr. Johnston teaches various subjects at local colleges and universities in order to learn things and to warp/delinearize young minds. Roger is also the author of the almost serious books, *Security Sound Bites: Important Ideas About Security from Smart-Ass, Dumb-Ass, and Kick-Ass Quotations* and *Devil's Dictionary of Security Terms*.